John

INTERPRETATION
BIBLE STUDIES

John

MARK A. MATSON

WESTMINSTER
JOHN KNOX PRESS
LOUISVILLE · KENTUCKY

Scripture quotations, unless otherwise indicated, are from the New Revised Standard Version of the Bible, copyright © 1989 by the Division of Christian Education of the National Council of the Churches of Christ in the U.S.A., and are used by permission.

The photographs on pages 10, 43, 55, 77, 87, and 122 are © Superstock, Inc. The photographs on pages 21, 94, and 113 are © PhotoDisc, Inc.

Book design by Sharon Adams
Cover design by Pam Poll
Cover illustration by Robert Stratton

First edition
Published by Westminster John Knox Press
Louisville, Kentucky

This book is printed on acid-free paper that meets the American National Standards Institute Z39.48 standard. ♾

PRINTED IN THE UNITED STATES OF AMERICA

08 09 10 11 — 10 9 8 7 6

Library of Congress Cataloging-in-Publication Data

Matson, Mark A., 1951–
  John / Mark A. Matson.—1st ed.
    p. cm. — (Interpretation Bible Studies)
  Includes bibliographical references.
  ISBN-13: 978-0-664-22580-3 (alk. paper)
  ISBN-10: 0-664-22580-2 (alk. paper)
    1. Bible. N.T. John—Criticism, interpretation, etc. 2. Bible. N.T. John—Textbooks.
I. Title. II. Series.

BS2615.52 .M28 2002
226.5'06—dc21   2001056765

Contents

Series Introduction

The Bible has long been revered for its witness to God's presence and redeeming activity in the world; its message of creation and judgment, love and forgiveness, grace and hope; its memorable characters and stories; its challenges to human life; and its power to shape faith. For generations people have found in the Bible inspiration and instruction, and, for nearly as long, commentators and scholars have assisted students of the Bible. This series, Interpretation Bible Studies (IBS), continues that great heritage of scholarship with a fresh approach to biblical study.

Designed for ease and flexibility of use for either personal or group study, IBS helps readers not only to learn about the history and theology of the Bible, understand the sometimes difficult language of biblical passages, and marvel at the biblical accounts of God's activity in human life, but also to accept the challenge of the Bible's call to discipleship. IBS offers sound guidance for deepening one's knowledge of the Bible and for faithful Christian living in today's world.

IBS was developed out of three primary convictions. First, the Bible is the church's scripture and stands in a unique place of authority in Christian understanding. Second, good scholarship helps readers understand the truths of the Bible and sharpens their perception of God speaking through the Bible. Third, deep knowledge of the Bible bears fruit in one's ethical and spiritual life.

Each IBS volume has ten brief units of key passages from a book of the Bible. By moving through these units, readers capture the sweep of the whole biblical book. Each unit includes study helps, such as maps, photos, definitions of key terms, questions for reflection, and suggestions for resources for further study. In the back of each volume is a Leader's Guide that offers helpful suggestions on how to use IBS.

The Interpretation Bible Studies series grows out of the well-known Interpretation commentaries (John Knox Press), a series that helps preachers and teachers in their preparation. Although each IBS volume bears a deep kinship to its companion Interpretation commentary, IBS can stand alone. The reader need not be familiar with the Interpretation commentary to benefit from IBS. However, those who want to discover even more about the Bible will benefit by consulting Interpretation commentaries too.

Through the kind of encounter with the Bible encouraged by the Interpretation Bible Studies, the church will continue to discover God speaking afresh in the scriptures.

Introduction to John

Among the Gospels, the Fourth Gospel stands out because of its structure, its tone, and the picture it gives of Jesus' self-revelation. It has been called the "spiritual Gospel" because it deals so clearly with issues of the origination and destination of Jesus from heaven and the crucial role of faith in Jesus' life. But that should not dispose one to think of it as somehow less concerned with the presentation of Jesus as a man who interacts with people in his time. John presents a compelling account of Jesus' life and the conflicts that arise in response to his claims about his relationship with God. Alongside the spiritual interpretation of Jesus is a story of growing conflict, of differing choices about how to understand Jesus, and finally of his self-sacrifice in the name of love for all humanity.

A quick look at the structure of John gives us some idea of the main emphases of the Gospel:

1. Before the plot begins, the author frames the story of Jesus with a theological prologue in which the reader learns that this man Jesus is the preexistent Word of God, partner in the very creation of the world. And we learn that the incarnation is an attempt to reconcile creation with God, to bring light to darkness. But that attempt will result in a tragic rejection—tragic because those who refuse to believe in Jesus reject God.

2. The initial account of Jesus' life is punctuated by a series of miracles that are called "signs." This term is provocative; it suggests that these miracles point to a deeper reality than simple miraculous activity. Although the signs continue throughout the Gospel (the resurrection and the story of the catch of fish that follows the resurrection must be counted as signs), most are found in the early part of the Gospel, and so the first eleven chapters are often called the "book of signs."

3. Interspersed between the signs, and especially after the final supper, are long dialogues or discourses that Jesus engages in with various individuals. In these discourses, Jesus makes a number of dramatic interpretations of who he is and how people should react to him. These sayings are obviously self-revelatory, in contrast to the sayings of Jesus in the other Gospels. Often the sayings in John are cast in metaphors that begin with "I am": for example, "I am the bread come down from heaven"; "I am the light of the world."

> "[John] requires both belief and infinite painstaking study. John is a treasure of the church as a document of faith. It is betrayed if it is interpreted as a charter of complacent exclusiveness or an instrument of divine wrath. The Evangelist's profoundest hope is that he has written a book calculated to bring about belief in Jesus Christ in fuller measure. It must always be preached and taught in the church in that Johannine spirit."—Sloyan, *John*, Interpretation, 233.

4. As the story progresses, it reveals a growing opposition to Jesus on the part of a group called "the Jews." This group, which is neither the same as the Jewish people nor the same as the leadership of the Jews, increases its resistance to both the message and the person of Jesus. Even before the final Passover they plot to kill Jesus.

5. After the raising of Lazarus in chapter 11, the focus shifts to Jesus' anticipated death. This death, in John's Gospel, is framed as a "glorification." There is little sense of tragedy in the death, for this is always understood to be the destiny of Jesus. In this death on the cross, Jesus' mission will be made clear. Furthermore, with his death Jesus returns to God. The end of the Gospel is thus linked to the Prologue.

6. The life of Jesus is not told as consisting of a single year. Instead, Jesus is seen to be returning to Jerusalem a number of times. John understands his active ministry to have lasted at least three years. The recurring trips to Jerusalem also punctuate another feature of Jesus' story—it finds its geographical focus to be the center of Jewish religious life, the Temple, and it is structured around the Jewish religious calendar and its festivals.

This rather striking structure sets John apart from the other three Gospels, the Synoptic Gospels (called "synoptic" because they are "seen together"). How should we understand the relationship between John and the Synoptics? On the one hand, it is clear that all four Gospels tell the story of Jesus, with a major focus being his crucifixion and resurrection. And in all the Gospels, Jesus performs miracles and faces opposition from the religious establishment of his time. On the other hand, the Synoptics and John tell the story of Jesus in such strikingly different ways that some explanation must be made for the similarities and the differences between them. The scope of this study is not large enough to engage these issues of relationship in a practical manner. My own conclusion is that John is independent of the other Gospels: the Fourth Gospel is not literarily dependent on any of the other Gospels but is based instead on oral traditions. But this conclusion is not crucial for a reading of the Gospel. In this study, more often than not, comparison with the other Gospels will be made only to cast in sharp relief the distinctive nature of John's story of Jesus.

Who, Where, and When?

The distinctive structure of John's Gospel has led to a number of theories about sources and editorial influence on the final document. In addition to the question of whether John might have drawn on the Synoptics as a source for the writing is the question of whether one can detect earlier versions that preceded the final Gospel. Most common in such theories is the suggestion that there existed an early narrative, without the discourses, that might be called a "signs Gospel." I think it quite possible that our Gospel may have gone through multiple stages

> ### *Who Wrote the Gospel?*
>
> Tradition holds that the Gospel of John was written by John the son of Zebedee, one of the Twelve. Some, however, believe that the one called "John the Elder"—thought to have written the epistles of John—wrote the Gospel. There are other theories of authorship as well.

of development, but again, this question is up in the air and is not crucial for a reading of the present canonical Gospel. Accordingly, the question has found little or no expression in this study.

A similar response can be issued to certain introductory questions: Who wrote the Gospel, when, where, and to whom? These are interesting questions, although no definitive answers can be given. And, ultimately, the attempts to answer the questions may lead the reader astray from hearing the central Gospel message. Accordingly, in the study that follows little attention is paid to these questions. Because it is difficult to know precisely who wrote the Gospel, I generally prefer to refer to the Gospel as the Fourth Gospel and to the author as the Fourth Evangelist. However, I also refer to the Gospel as "John's Gospel" and occasionally to John as author, although this should not be taken as a judgment on the actual author.

It is true, as I discuss in the last chapter, that the author of the Gospel claims to be an eyewitness, the "disciple whom Jesus loved" (or "the beloved disciple"). If we take the final chapter of John seriously, we must at least engage this claim in our understanding of its assertion to truthfulness. But, as I point out, that does not make it clear who the beloved disciple was—this is still a matter of debate.

The other questions—date of authorship, place, audience—are even less clear and less important. The writing of the Fourth Gospel is frequently placed within a community of believers who were distinct, even cut off, from the rest of Christianity. It is, then, conceived of as a sectarian document. I am not convinced of this. It claims something quite different—that is, it claims to be an attempt to produce faith (20:30–31), which would be unusual if it were written by and for a sectarian group that already believed in Jesus. It is also frequently believed to have arisen outside Palestine, but in many ways John's Gospel pays more attention to Jewish geography and calendar issues than do the other Gospels. It is, in effect, more Jewish and more Palestinian than other Gospels. Finally, the Gospel is often considered to be a very late composition, well into the latter part of the first century and possibly into the beginning of the second. Again, I find these arguments less than compelling. But whatever the suppositions about these introductory issues, they generally do not lead the reader to greater insight into the message of the Gospel. That message stands on its own, and it is the developing force of that message that I have tried to emphasize in the study.

> For further reading about the Gospel according to John, see Gerard Sloyan, *John*, Interpretation (Louisville, Ky.: John Knox Press, 1988); William Barclay, *The Gospel of John*, vols. 1 and 2, New Daily Study Bible (Louisville, Ky.: Westminster John Knox Press, 2001).

Theological Viewpoints

More important to the study of the Fourth Gospel is an awareness of some significant theological viewpoints by which the author interprets the story of Jesus. Many of these become apparent as this study of the Gospel explores them. It may be worthwhile, however, to highlight some of the more significant features that should be kept in mind throughout the study of the Gospel.

The first feature is the strongly dualistic perspective of the author. The Fourth Evangelist frequently casts the mission of Jesus in terms of sharply contrasted opposites. The most striking is the light/dark motif. Jesus is the light; he comes to a world of darkness. The dualism of light and dark corresponds to the separation of heaven from the world. This dualism can be seen in some of the Gospel's dialogues where opposition to Jesus is cast as a lie versus truth, as the rulers of this world versus God. It used to be asserted that this was a sign of the influence of Greek or Hellenistic thought on John's Gospel. The discovery of the Dead Sea Scrolls, however, makes it clear that such dualisms were common in Judaism of the first century as well.

The second feature is the strong opposition to Jesus by "the Jews." The prologue begins with the comment that the Word "came to what was his own, and his own people did not accept him." This viewpoint informs the entire Gospel, being the basis for much of the plot. Jesus moves in and out of Jerusalem in part because of the opposition of "the Jews," and many of his discourses engage this opposition. In the passion story, the opposition of "the Jews" leads to his death—indeed, it is quite proper to see them in this Gospel actually crucifying Jesus. But, as I discuss in Unit 9, it is a challenge to identify exactly who "the Jews" are. The term does not simply represent Judaism, since Jesus affirms much of the tradition. Nor does it refer to all the people who are Jews, since many of these do believe. Instead, it must be seen as John's literary creation, shorthand so to speak, to refer to the rejection of Jesus by "his own." Because the term is a literary device and should not be taken to mean all of Judaism, I bracket the term throughout this study in quotation marks—"the Jews"—in order to emphasize this distinction.

Finally, a third feature is the Fourth Evangelist's understanding of Jesus as originating "from heaven," the place to which he will return. This descent/ascent concept pervades the Gospel and informs its portrayal of Jesus' relationship with God. Jesus has a prior relationship with God and has been "sent" by God into the world. As

 Want to Know More?

About leading Bible study groups? See Roberta Hestenes, *Using the Bible in Groups* (Philadelphia: Westminster Press, 1983); Christine Blair, *The Art of Teaching the Bible* (Louisville, Ky.: Geneva Press, 2001).

About the differences between John and the Synoptic Gospels? See William Barclay, *The Gospel of John*, vol. 1, New Daily Study Bible (Louisville, Ky.: Westminster John Knox Press, 2001), 2–5.

About the development of the Gospels? See William M. Ramsay, *The Westminster Guide to the Books of the Bible* (Louisville, Ky.: Westminster John Knox Press, 1994), 289–316; John Barton, *How the Bible Came to Be* (Louisville, Ky.: Westminster John Knox Press, 1997), 18–22, 44–46; Archibald M. Hunter, *Introducing the New Testament*, 3d rev. ed. (Philadelphia: Westminster Press, 1972), 23–26.

About the content or themes of each Gospel? See Duncan S. Ferguson, *Bible Basics: Mastering the Content of the Bible* (Louisville, Ky.: Westminster John Knox Press, 1995), 57–65; Hunter, *Introducing the New Testament*, 37–70.

a result, Jesus is always a bit more divine in this Gospel than in the Synoptics. While the author is at great pains to affirm Jesus' humanity, his extra-earthly origin is always in view: Jesus is intimately related to God, knows about God's will, and knows his own future and his destination.

In this study I have tried to focus on key developments of John's story of Jesus. I believe that, as the conclusion in 20:30–31 indicates, this Gospel was written as an argument for belief. Hence, I have tried to point out how John lets that argument build in the course of the narrative and the discourses. The author of the Fourth Gospel often builds the argument by repetition and reference. Frequently, similar ideas are repeated or themes that were broached early in the Gospel (especially in the prologue) find their fulfillment in the narrative. I have tried to focus attention on these internal cross-references. In other words, the major thrust of this study is to better understand the evangelist's own purpose in writing the Fourth Gospel.

I am indebted to my former professor D. Moody Smith, at Duke University, for helping sharpen my inquiry into the Fourth Gospel and excite my interest in a serious study of all the Gospels, and to the late Dr. Beauford Bryant, my seminary professor, for beginning my interest in the Gospels. I also am grateful to my students from classes on John's Gospel at both Milligan College and Emmanuel School of Religion, who helped me think through some of the issues presented in this study. My research assistant, Jason Evans, provided many helpful comments on style and readability, as did my colleague Dr. Craig Farmer.

Note: For those who would like more information about some of the issues in the Gospel, a good commentary would be useful. You will want access to the Interpretation commentary *John*, by Gerard Sloyan (Atlanta: John Knox Press, 1988); *Interpretation* is the basis for this Bible study series. Another very readable commentary is *John*, by D. Moody Smith Jr. (Nashville: Abingdon Press, 1999). Far more extensive but still the classic in Johannine studies is Raymond Brown's two-volume commentary in the Anchor Bible series. A good Bible dictionary will also be very helpful. Throughout this study I have used the New Revised Standard Version (NRSV) of the Bible, except when I have translated a text myself for emphasis.

Testimony Concerning the Word

The Fourth Gospel is a story about Jesus. But it is also constructed as an argument for belief. We should, perhaps, always read the beginning of the Gospel with the author's purpose in mind: "Jesus did many other signs in the presence of his disciples, which are not written in this book. But these are written so that you may come to believe that Jesus is the Christ, the Son of God, and that through believing you may have life in his name" (John 20:30–31). The opening of the book focuses especially on who Jesus is, his relationship with the God of Israel, and the purpose of his mission on earth. It is a thoroughly theological introduction but at the same time an introduction aimed at preparing the argument for belief.

The Prologue (1:1–18)

John's version of the story of Jesus does not begin with the birth of Jesus (as do Matthew and Luke), nor with the initial ministry (as does Mark), but rather with a poem. The Fourth Evangelist has used a deliberate literary form, a philosophical reflection, to preface the Gospel, rather than proceeding directly into a narrative. In doing so, the author signals something of his purpose: this Gospel is to be a reflection on the importance of Jesus, not just a narration of the life of Jesus. By using poetic language, the Fourth Evangelist sets Jesus outside time and human experience—Jesus truly has a cosmic and eternal significance. But this is not a poem that is entirely timeless either, for it interacts with the Jesus of history as well. Time and eternity meet and interpret each other in the Prologue to John.

7

At the same time, the opening poem carefully anticipates a number of major themes that resonate throughout the Gospel: the singular relationship of Jesus with God; the sharp division between those who believe and those who do not (as light and darkness); the revelation of glory that was the life of Jesus; the importance of the incarnation as an event in history; the rejection of Jesus that is the indication of the darkness that has enveloped humanity; and the special role that testimony and evidence play in the argument for the reader to believe in Jesus. This poem, then, is a carefully constructed rhetorical device designed to set the stage for the narrative to follow.

The basic meaning of the Prologue is clear. Jesus Christ was not just a prophet or a savior but was, indeed, the incarnation of the very Word of God, the active power of God involved in creating the world and bringing life. Thus Jesus, who was in human form, was God manifest, God come near, God come to bring humanity back to God. But while the basic meaning is clear, the poetic language used presents difficulties. These difficulties, however, only invite the reader to contemplate the meaning more.

The Opening Poem

There has often been discussion over whether the opening poem was part of the original Gospel story. Its poetic quality alone might tend to raise the question of whether it was added onto the story as a late addition. This raises some important questions about the history of the composition of the Gospel. But how the Gospel came into being need not detain us. Instead, the final form of the Fourth Gospel as found in our current canon of scripture situates the introductory poem as a framing device to draw us into the story that follows and to help interpret for the reader the meaning of Jesus' life.

A. Structure of the Poem

Three major impulses dominate this poem. The first is to identify the Word with God's creative and life-giving activity. The second is to speak of the incarnation of the Word in Jesus, an incarnation that revealed God's glory but that was rejected by much of humanity. The third is to emphasize the role of belief in the Word, based on testimony about Jesus. But how do these impulses in the poem actually develop?

One can speak of the poem as being formed in three major units, but with interruptions. The first major unit, verses 1–5, deals with the Word, its relationship with God, and its role in the very act of creation. In the second major unit, verses 9–13, the theme is the Word's role in the world. And in the third major unit, verses 14–18, the theme is the testimony of the community of faith to the Word's life as a human being. The flow, then, seems to be from a cosmic role to an earthly mission and then, finally, to the specific relationship with believers.

The first unit of the Prologue begins outside history and beyond the realm of human experience: "In the beginning was the Word, and the Word was in the presence of God, and the Word was God. He was in the beginning in the presence of God. All things came into being through him, and apart from him not a single thing which has happened took place. In him was life, and this life was the light of humanity. And the light shines in the darkness, and the darkness did not overcome it" (John 1:1–5, author's translation).

It is apparent that the author of the Fourth Gospel intended for the reader to "hear" the opening words of Genesis echoed in the opening verse of this poem: "In the beginning . . ." Once one makes the connection with the creation story in Genesis, other images in the Prologue begin to make sense. In Genesis, God "speaks" the world into being; John refers to the Word, the *logos*, as being the agent of all creation. In Genesis, light is the first thing created, and God then separates light and dark; John speaks of the Word as light that shines in the darkness. The opening verses of the Prologue, then, are in dialogue with the well-known opening verses of Genesis and serve to frame the story of Jesus in terms of God's creative impulse before time began.

But, at the same time, the first unit of the poem anticipates the drama of the life and death of Jesus: "The light shines in the darkness, and the darkness did not overcome it." This final verse introduces a battle between darkness and light that is not inherently part of the creation story. The darkness in Genesis is night, or perhaps the preexisting state before light was created. But John understands darkness as a spiritual quality, in direct opposition to light. Moreover, the poem suggests that the darkness has tried to overcome the light, to vanquish it, but has been unable to do so. Is this not the first hint of the passion story? If so, then John has already pointed to the incarnation in the first phrasing of the poem, for the death of Christ presumes a human incarnation.

> "In an important sense the opening of the Gospel is as much about the origins of the believers to whom it is addressed as it is about the origins of Jesus. He came forth from God as Word or Life or Light (vv. 1–5), says the omniscient narrator, before he became flesh to dwell among *us*."—Sloyan, *John*, Interpretation, 14.

But now, instead of moving directly to the incarnation, the poem is seemingly interrupted by the introduction of John the Baptist, identified simply as "John." This John is defined as a witness to the light and not the light itself. This distinction clearly indicates that the author was already thinking about the human Jesus in the last sentence of the previous unit; the reference to John the Baptist brings us suddenly to the historical situation of Jesus. More important, it indicates how fundamental the role of persuasion is in the mind of the author. John is a witness to the true nature of Jesus as the Word and the light. Witnesses are crucial to making a convincing proof of a historical event. The whole Gospel is thus aimed at persuading the reader of Jesus' nature and person.

There is a hint here that the author of the Fourth Gospel knew of a possible misapprehension of who John the Baptist was. Note that the Fourth Evangelist goes to great lengths to differentiate between John the Baptist and Jesus. John the Baptist is a witness to the light but not the light itself. In 1:15, John the Baptist is again a witness and declares his subordination to Jesus; in 1:20, John the Baptist explicitly proclaims, "I am not the Christ"; and in 3:25–30, John the Baptist again reiterates that he is not the Christ and that as Jesus' ministry grows, John's own importance will decrease. The evangelist seems intent on making John the Baptist's role clear: he is a forerunner and a witness to the Christ but not the Christ himself.

Jesus' baptism

The second major unit of thought picks up the previous theme of the Word as the light of the world: "He was the true light, which, upon coming into the world, enlightens every person. He was in the world, and though the world came into being through him, yet the world did not know him. He came to his own, but his own did not receive him. But as many as did receive him, he gave to those who believed in his name authority to become children of God. These are born, not from blood nor from the will of flesh, nor from the will of a man, but from God" (John 1:9–13, author's translation).

The concept of the incarnation of the Word is even stronger in the second unit, although it is not explicit. "He was in the world," and "He came to his own" suggest the entry of the Word, the true light, into prosaic human events. The author has introduced a new concept, "the world." Is this a reference to human events, to history, or

10

is there a deeper meaning to the term? For John, "the world" carries a multiplicity of meanings. It is the object of God's love, not God's judgment (3:16–19), yet the world has judged itself by rejecting the light. Jesus came to bring life to the world (6:33), although he is not "of this world" (8:23). He came from the Father into the world and will return to the Father by leaving the world (16:28). The world is the object of Jesus' mission and yet rejects him and hates his followers (17:14). For the Fourth Evangelist, then, the term *the world* is the locus of fallen humanity but the object of a mission from God. It is a distinct "place" and "time." So, in the second unit of the Prologue, the entry of the Word into the world signifies the incarnation of Jesus. And, again, it anticipates the fundamental conflict that finds its completion at the cross: the world, and especially his own people, rejects the Word.

There is a sketchy narrative structure in this unit of the poem: Jesus comes into the world, but the world is ignorant about his role in creation. This appears to be a general statement, perhaps referring to the Gentile world who did not know the God of the patriarchs, the true God of creation. But John goes on to say that Jesus came to his own, possibly implying the Jewish people. And these people are not ignorant of God; rather, they reject the Word of God. Here is the drama of the life of Jesus—that he was rejected by the very people who had been given the revelation of God. Finally, however, God fashions his own people not by blood lineage but by using those who accept Jesus and God's work in the incarnation.

The second unit of the poem reiterates the overriding concern of the Gospel—that of persuading the reader to believe Jesus is God incarnate. The final phrase makes clear the central issue at stake: belief. Belief (the Greek word *pistis*) has at its root the idea of persuasion: one believes when one is persuaded about the reality of a fact. Here the author counts belief in the name of Jesus to be so powerful and so crucial that it can create a rebirth as a child of God. But what does it mean "to believe in his name"? This, of course, is the rest of the story—that which the Gospel will make clear. For now, however, the author plants the seed that this is the crucial issue at stake.

With the third unit, the implication of the incarnation is made completely clear: "And the Word became flesh and dwelt among us, and we beheld his glory, glory as the only begotten from God, full of grace and truth. John testified concerning him and has cried out: 'This was the one of whom I said: "The one coming after me has come into being before me, for he was first."' Because from his fullness all of us have received even grace from grace; for the law was given from Moses, but grace and truth came through Jesus Christ. No one has ever beheld God; the only begotten of God, who is in the bosom of the Father, has made him known" (John 1:14–18, author's translation). With the clear statement of the incarnation of the Word, we learn that Jesus is the physical manifestation of God, the only begotten (or unique) Son of God, who shows God's glory as it has never before been seen.

> **Son of Man**
>
> "So, Jesus is all of these: Lamb of God, God's Chosen One, Messiah, the man spoken of by Moses in the Law and by the prophets, King of Israel, and far greater than John the Baptist. . . . Surely Jesus is the Messiah in the sense that all of these titles suggest. Surely he is greater than John the Baptist. But his real identity is tucked away in the meaning of this expression, Son of Man."—Kysar, *John: The Maverick Gospel*, 39.

Again, the author returns to the importance of John the Baptist's witness about Jesus. It is not clear whether John's testimony is contained only in verse 15 or extends all the way to verse 18. If the latter, then John the Baptist is shown affirming what the Fourth Evangelist has already stated, that Jesus shows the glory of God uniquely, even more powerfully than Moses.

As one examines the structure of the poem and how it develops its ideas, it is clear that recurrent themes are developed in successive "waves." That the Word came into world to bring light and life to humanity is introduced vaguely in the first unit ("The light shines in the darkness, and the darkness did not overcome it"), then a bit more strongly in the second unit ("He was in the world, and the world came into being through him; yet the world did not know him"), then clearly in the third unit ("And the Word became flesh and lived among us"). Similarly, the interest in persuasion is introduced with John the Baptist ("He came as a witness to testify to the light, so that all might believe through him"), is raised a second time in the second unit ("to all who . . . believed in his name, he gave power to become children of God"), and is reiterated in the third unit ("John testified to him"). And the passion narrative is anticipated throughout. In the first unit, a simple allusion ("and the darkness did not overcome it") points to it. In the second unit, the anticipation is stronger still ("his own people did not accept him"). The author does not have a linear approach to presenting ideas but repeats them in varying forms, establishing images that anticipate and interpret the narrative to follow.

12

B. The Background of John's Metaphor of "the Word"

It is apparent that the Fourth Evangelist is making adept use of images and concepts in his Prologue, images that draw on preexisting ideas and, by reference, add to the readers' understanding of the Christ event. (I have already noted how the opening verses draw on the first chapter of Genesis.) This use of previous literature and widely known concepts is both metaphorical and allusive. This is particularly true of John's term *the Word*, which is profoundly metaphorical. But against what previous literature or concepts should the reader compare this term in order to draw out its full meaning?

There are numerous instances in the Old Testament where God speaks. In addition to "speaking" the creation, God speaks through the prophets; the prophetic oracles are often called the "word of the Lord" (cf. Jer. 1:4 and many other instances). In contrast, the "word of the Lord" is often simply a term used for the Law, the Torah (see, for instance, Isa. 2:3, where the word of the Lord is directly paralleled with the Torah). But both uses lack the free-standing cosmological quality that the Fourth Evangelist understands in his use of the term.

It has often been suggested that the origin of the idea of *logos* in John's Gospel lies in Greek philosophy, especially Stoicism. In Stoicism, the *logos* is the underlying quality that unites God, humans, and the created order. The "seminal word" (*logos spermatikos*) is said to be that element of God which permeates the universe but is especially present in human beings because they are rational. Since the word *logos* can mean rational thinking and order as well as the spoken word, this connection between the order of nature and God becomes cosmological—the creative force in the world is

> **Stoicism**
>
> Stoicism was a school of philosophy founded in Athens by Zeno (335–263 B.C.) that held the entire universe was a living creature animated by the divine *Logos* (reason or mind). Since the *Logos* ruled everyone and pervaded everything, everything that happened in the universe was governed by the law of nature or providence. And since everything was determined, the only way individuals could control their lives was to control how they reacted to external events. Control of oneself became the avenue through which humans showed their freedom and superiority to fortune.

"the word" (lowercase). But in John's Gospel, "the Word" (capitalized, as a divine presence) is not something that is independently present in the world or even in human beings. Rather, "the Word" is uniquely applied to Jesus as God's only Son. If John wanted his readers to compare his Prologue with Stoicism, then it was for the purpose of producing a comparison of dissimilarity, not similarity.

A more likely possibility for the conceptual background of John's use of the term *the Word* is the wisdom traditions of Israel. These traditions are found in the book of Proverbs in the Old Testament and in the books of Sirach and Wisdom of Solomon in the Apocrypha. In the Jewish Wisdom literature, God's wisdom is seen as an independent quality and one that is involved in the creation and sustenance of the world:

> The LORD created me [wisdom] at the beginning of his work,
>> the first of his acts of long ago.
> Ages ago I was set up,
>> at the first, before the beginning of the earth.
>
> (Prov. 8:22–23)

> When he established the heavens, I [wisdom] was there,
>> when he drew a circle on the face of the deep, . . .
> when he marked out the foundations of the earth,
>> then I was beside him, like a master worker.
>
> (Prov. 8:27, 29, 30)

> I [wisdom] came forth from the mouth of the Most High,
>> and covered the earth like a mist.
> I dwelt in the highest heavens,
>> and my throne was in a pillar of cloud.
>
> (Sir. 24:3–4)

> With you [God] is wisdom, she who knows your works
> and was present when you made the world.
>
> (Wis. 9:9)

This wisdom is seen as a life-giving quality for those who draw on it:

> For whoever finds me [wisdom] finds life
> and obtains favor from the LORD.
>
> (Prov. 8:35)

> Because of her [wisdom] I shall have immortality.
>
> (Wis. 8:13)

Wisdom is also seen as the source of light and revelation:

> For she is the revelation of eternal light,
> a spotless mirror of the working of God,
> and an image of his goodness.

(Wis. 7:26)

The author of John, then, seems to be using traditions about wisdom already well known to those familiar with the scriptures and Jewish traditions and has used this concept to interpret Jesus from an eternal and cosmological perspective.

Testimonies of John the Baptist (1:19–34)

After the Prologue, the Fourth Gospel begins its narrative with John the Baptist. But the reader does not first hear of John's preaching in the wilderness, nor of his baptizing. Indeed, the reader must read a bit further to find that this John is indeed the Baptizer (vv. 25, 28, 31–34). Instead, the Baptist is introduced first by his words of "testimony," a testimony that declares that he is not the Christ, not Elijah, not the prophet. Only then does he preach using Isaiah 40:3, a quotation the other Gospels also place on his lips.

John's witness is actually manifold and, at the very opening verses of the Gospel, informs the reader of crucial information:

1. At the outset, John identifies himself to the Jewish leadership in terms of what he is not. This emphatic negation, given in response to specific questions, serves to anticipate who Jesus is. If John is not the Christ, who is? If John is not the prophet, who is? If John is not Elijah, who is? At the same time, the questions indicate that the Jewish leadership should be able to recognize who Jesus is, since they are clearly looking forward to the coming of the Christ. John's initial witness, then, is negative but at the same time sets the stage for the positive identification to come.

2. That an expectation of Jesus' coming is the theme in John's witness is made clear in the second exchange. When asked why he baptizes, John responds that he baptizes in water even while one greater is coming after him. Again, John deflects identification of himself toward the coming one. And the curious statement

"I baptize with water" suggests that someone else will baptize with another medium—that of the Holy Spirit.

3. On seeing Jesus, John immediately confesses Jesus' identity: "Here is the Lamb of God who takes away the sin of the world!" Moreover, lest there be any doubt, John states that this is the one of whom he has been speaking, the one who will come after him. It is certainly clear that this reference is meant to reflect Jesus' special role as the savior of the world. The "Lamb of God" has often been taken to refer to the paschal lamb that is sacrificed at Passover. Especially since—in the Fourth Gospel's chronology—Jesus dies on the day the Passover lamb is sacrificed, this has been a tempting explanation for the term. But the paschal lamb was never a sacrifice (Passover was a feast, not an atonement sacrifice), and it is never represented as taking away sin. More suggestive is the connection with Isaiah 53, where the Suffering Servant of Israel is likened to a lamb led to slaughter. This servant is said to be "an offering for sin" (Isa. 53:10). The background for John's term *Lamb of God* may well also lie in Old Testament passages that speak of the offering of the lamb (Exod. 29:38–46, for the daily Temple offerings, or Lev. 4:32, for an individual's sin offering). But the Fourth Evangelist does not explain the term; instead, it becomes one of a variety of terms for Jesus that accumulate and create a tapestry of concepts for the reader to use in the subsequent story.

Want to Know More?

About the word *logos* in John? See William Barclay, *New Testament Words* (Louisville, Ky.: Westminster John Knox Press, 1974), 178–188.

About the titles for Jesus in John 1:19–51? See Robert Kysar, *John: The Maverick Gospel*, rev. ed. (Louisville, Ky.: Westminster John Knox Press, 1993), 35–40.

4. The Fourth Gospel does not explicitly relate Jesus' baptism. Instead, the reader is left to infer, perhaps by comparison with the other Gospels, that John has baptized Jesus. But John does relate the coming of the Holy Spirit, descending like a dove on Jesus. John goes on to say that this person on whom the Spirit descended will himself baptize with the Holy Spirit. The baptism received from Jesus, then, will be qualitatively different from and better than that received from John the Baptist. This, too, seems to anticipate Jesus' ministry and, more important, the sending of the Paraclete following Jesus' death (cf. John 16:5–15; 20:22).

5. Finally, John makes a solemn testimony that Jesus is the Son of God. This echoes the statement in the Prologue that Jesus is the

only Son of the Father (1:14, 18). The language identifies Jesus as more than a prophet, indeed, the very and only Son of God. The Prologue anticipates John the Baptist's testimony, and John's testimony affirms the language of the Prologue.

The First Disciples (1:35–51)

After John the Baptist's witness to Jesus, the Gospel turns to a short series of scenes in which Jesus begins to gather disciples. These disciples are drawn initially from the followers of John the Baptist, and their impulse to follow Jesus is based on John the Baptist's statements about him. Because of John the Baptist's testimony, Andrew confesses that Jesus is the Messiah and brings his brother Simon Peter to Jesus as well. This scene is followed a second day with Jesus' calling of Philip. Philip then testifies to Nathanael, who perceives that Jesus is the Son of God and confesses this to Jesus.

This short narrative serves to link John the Baptist with Jesus' disciples. But more important, we see the significance of testimony and acknowledgment of who Jesus is. He is immediately understood to be the Messiah by Andrew and the Son of God by Nathanael. These, too, become witnesses to Jesus. And they fulfill the mission for which Jesus came, that people should believe. But Jesus' statement of amazement that Nathanael believes on the basis of only a prophetic word suggests that belief will not be as easy for others. And Jesus' statement that Nathanael will see even greater things anticipates the signs that will come.

The stage is set. Jesus has come to his own, and some of his own have understood who he is and believe. They testify to his nature. But the reader is also aware that rejection and disbelief are possible.

The Titles of Jesus

The opening chapter of the Fourth Gospel prepares the reader for the story to come, a story filled with signs and discourses, a tale of conflict and death. By providing the reader a cosmic perspective of Jesus and using language of rhetoric and persuasion, the author is actively engaging the reader to make a decision about who Jesus really is. One more element in this effort to frame the discussion in terms of the decision of faith is a striking feature of the opening chapter of the Fourth Gospel: the author uses a wide variety of metaphors and titles to refer to Jesus, so that, by the end of the chapter, one has the impression that Jesus is, indeed, all in all. The range of titles is almost dizzying in its scope. A quick review shows the breadth and inclusiveness of the terms used to set the scene for Jesus:

- In the Prologue, Jesus is identified in a cluster of metaphors that are cosmic and foundational in nature: the Word, the life, the light.
- The second group of titles assigned to Jesus identify him in terms of God; they are relational terms: (only begotten) Son of the Father, the Son of God, and the Elect of God.
- The third group of titles are functional terms that identify some aspect of Jesus' role, especially involving certain expectations in Israel: Christ (v. 20); the Hebrew form of Christ, Messiah (v. 41); the King of Israel; and Rabbi.
- Finally, Jesus is referred to with certain prophetic or apocalyptic terms: the Lamb of God, the Son of Man.

As the Fourth Evangelist closes the opening section of the Gospel, he has prepared his readers to read the story with knowledge that is indeed revelatory. There is no doubt who Jesus is, and there are hints of the conflict to come. The blueprint of the argument has been made clear. What follows is the construction of the case for belief in Jesus, a case confirmed by signs, further testimony, and the testimony of Jesus himself.

? Questions for Reflection

1. Do you think it is significant that the Gospel of John doesn't begin with a birth narrative, as Matthew and Luke do?
2. Compare John 1:1–18 to Genesis 1:1–2:3. What themes appear in both accounts? Why do you think the author may have wanted to make this comparison?
3. Why was it so important that John the Baptist's first witness to the coming of Christ was "negative," that is, "I am *not* the Christ"?
4. Read the list (page 18) of the different titles used to refer to Jesus. What were these different titles trying to convey about Jesus?

Of Signs and Faith

As the narrative of chapter 1 progresses, Jesus removes himself from the area around Jerusalem where he met John the Baptist and travels northward to Galilee (1:43). The next narrative unit is located, fittingly, in the Galilean region, in the town of Cana. Much later, in John 21:2, we learn that Nathanael was from Cana, so perhaps a geographical linkage may be drawn between the tradition about Nathanael in the closing words of chapter 1, in which Jesus promises Nathanael that he will see greater things to come, and this first "sign" of Jesus performed in Cana.

With the wedding at Cana, the ministry of Jesus enters a new phase, the phase of signs. Jesus' actions are dramatic and prophetic and in some way are meant to signify his nature and his mission. Signs, like testimony, are evidence that can be presented to persuade a reader to believe in Jesus as the incarnate Word of God.

Wedding at Cana (2:1–11)

John introduces the wedding scene with the chronological marker "on the third day." But this cannot be referring to the time from the encounter with John the Baptist; already more than three days have been specifically noted in chapter 1 (at least four days, perhaps more if we add the expected journey time to Galilee). While it is tempting to interpret this term symbolically in light of the resurrection on the third day, this seems uncalled for in the context of the narrative. The "third day" is probably used to refer to a short period of time after Jesus' promise to Nathanael that he will see greater signs. The time marker, then, may be a way of linking the disciples to the wedding story that follows. It is important for the sequential development of the story that the disciples are said to be invited to the wedding with Jesus, for the focus of the story is ultimately on their reaction to the miracle.

The setting for this sign is a wedding, and it is unique to the Gospel of John. The marriage setting may have an additional meaning for John as the Gospel writer interprets the life of Jesus in light of the Scriptures. Weddings were often understood to be indications of the coming of the messianic age, as Hosea 2:19–20; Isaiah 25:6–8; and Jeremiah 2:2 suggest.

> "Water is the great elixir of the Bible. One must have lived in a dry country for even a little while to know the force of the symbolism of thirst and its slaking, rivers and streams, dry river beds, and exhausted wells."—Sloyan, *John*, Interpretation, 36.

While the setting of a wedding feast may lead one to read some sense of fulfillment into the passage, one should guard against attaching an allegorical meaning to other aspects of the passage. The focus of the passage is primarily on Jesus performing a sign of his power. It has been suggested that the fact that Jesus uses stone jars meant for Jewish purification acts (i.e., for the *miqvah*, or immersion pool) is an indication that Jesus is somehow replacing Judaism. But the stone jars are merely part of the occasion for the miracle, and the story makes no judgment relative to the purification rites of Judaism. The reference to the stone jars may simply signify that these are large vessels, and hence the amount of wine produced is also prodigious.

The story proper is fairly straightforward and is miraculous. The wedding feast has run out of wine, and Jesus' mother informs him of this fact. While Mary's comment to Jesus is not phrased as a request to do something, such seems to be implied; Jesus then responds by directing that certain stone jars be filled with water. When the water is subsequently tasted, it has become good wine. Based on this, the disciples believe in Jesus.

Jesus' mother is introduced as a central character in the opening sentence of this account, but what follows is not a glowing or sentimental presentation. John's Gospel never identifies Jesus' mother as "Mary." It is an interesting feature of John's Gospel that she appears only early in the Gospel, as a main character in the first miracle story, and again at the end of the Gospel, when Jesus is on the cross (John 19:25–26). In both cases she is presented in close connection with the disciples. And in this story set in Cana, we find that the story concludes with Jesus and his mother and brothers and disciples departing together to Capernaum. And yet, while Jesus' mother is linked with the disciples, it is the disciples who are positively portrayed, whereas her role is somewhat ambiguous.

This ambiguous presentation of Jesus' mother is especially seen in the exchange between her and Jesus. In response to her informing him of the absence of wine, Jesus responds, "What concern is that to you and to me?" (3:4). This phrase is difficult to translate; it literally says, "what to me and to you?" It could mean "What have I done to you that you should bring this to me?" in which case it would indicate a strong sense of discord between Jesus and his mother. The context does not seem to point to this meaning. Instead, it is more likely meant to portray a mild form of distance—

Jesus turning water to wine

"Why are you bothering me with this?" Or it may be a general remark on Jesus' relationship with his mother, as the RSV reads: "O woman, what have you to do with me?" And as this translation shows, Jesus' form of address to his mother is "Woman." While this is Jesus' regular form of address to women in John's Gospel (compare 4:21; 8:10; 20:13; and 19:26, again with reference to Jesus' mother) and is also known in the other Gospels, it does seem a bit formal for a son addressing a mother. The response to his mother's information and the form of address together portray Jesus as distant from his mother.

Another confusing element in the exchange between Jesus and his mother is Jesus' statement "My hour has not yet come" (3:4). The term *my hour* or *the hour* is used frequently in the Fourth Gospel to refer to a future decisive time, and especially the passion, when Jesus' glory will be especially visible (see, for instance, John 7:30; 8:20; 12:23, 27; 13:1; 17:1). Used in the context of the Cana wedding, though, the term *my hour* is a bit confusing. Is Jesus saying, "Don't bother me now, since my time of glorification is not yet come?" If the time of glory is when Jesus will show his power, then why does he proceed here and elsewhere to perform miracles? And the Fourth Evangelist goes on to say that the miracle does, in fact, show Jesus' glory. So in what way is this not "his hour"?

There is a clear break between Jesus' exchange with his mother and the actions that follow. Despite the deflecting remark by Jesus, his mother initiates the action by telling the waiters to do whatever Jesus tells them to do. And Jesus then proceeds to direct the waiters to fill up the water jugs and present them to the steward. Jesus' mother and Jesus respond to each other as mother and son, despite the distancing language spoken between them. This disjunction between Jesus' interaction with his mother and what follows perhaps indicates that the cast of characters responds to Jesus in two different ways. On the one hand, Jesus takes care of the wedding feast as his mother requests, a feat the disciples (but not Jesus' mother) receive with belief in Jesus. On the other hand, the relationship between Jesus' mother and her son is not that of belief or discipleship, and as such her role is only that of "woman," a potential disciple but not yet one. Perhaps, then, this exchange is meant to look forward to the cross, when Jesus will assign her care to the beloved disciple—for only as a disciple, as a believer, will she receive life.

> "What was it about this particular sign that revealed for them the presence of God—of glory—in Jesus? Though the story does not spell it out for us, those who carried Old Testament promises in their hearts would have found its meaning clear: abundance of wine was one of the consistent Old Testament images for the joy of the messianic last days and the arrival of God's new age."—Gench, *Women and the Word,* 12.

In his *Interpretation* commentary, Gerard Sloyan says, "Only God's demands on Jesus, in other words, are to be heeded. Then the deed requested is done. . . . The disposition of events is always in divine hands, not human, Jesus seems to say in verse 4." Thus Jesus' question and statement "Woman, what concern is that to you and to me? My hour has not yet come" are meant to be discontinuous with this miracle and instead anticipate the cross, when Jesus' mother comes into the circle of disciples.

Beyond Jesus' exchange with his mother, the focus of the passage is on Jesus' willingness to perform a "sign." This is John's explicit way of talking about the miracle at Cana: "the first of his signs." A sign is an act that points beyond what takes place to something else, something more significant. Jesus' miracle at Cana points to his identity. The author points out that with this sign Jesus "revealed his glory," which is a key theme in the Fourth Gospel. By showing his glory, Jesus is actually displaying that he is the preexistent Word, the Son of God.

The word *glory* (or *splendor*) is used extensively in John and carries much power. Implicit in the word is the idea of the intensity of God's own presence. Thus, at the Sinai, God's presence among God's people is called "the glory of the Lord," a glory that leaves an image on Moses' face even after departing from the divine presence. (Exod. 24:15–17; 34:29–35). Glory, then, is a signification of the presence of the divine. Jesus shows his glory in those cases where he demonstrates his divinity, and he is ultimately "glorified" (clothed in splendor) when he is raised from the dead after his passion.

The striking result of this sign in Cana, however, is that his disciples believe in him. Here at the conclusion of the story is the essential point about this sign and all signs: that they serve as evidence of Jesus' identity and that certain individuals may, based on this evidence, come to belief in Jesus. Throughout the Fourth Gospel, signs point to Jesus' divinity. But they are understood as such only by those who choose to see them, who choose to be convinced of his identity.

The Temple Incident (2:13–25)

The Fourth Gospel again shows its unique approach with the placement of the Temple incident early in the ministry of Jesus. In all the other Gospels, this disruptive action in the Temple occurs in the last week of Jesus' life, just after he enters Jerusalem. Like the other Gospels, the setting in John is the Passover week. But John's Gospel seems to know of many times Jesus went to Jerusalem for Passover and thus portrays at least a three-year ministry, rather than what appears to be a one-year ministry in the other Gospels. It is possible that John records better information about Jesus' life. The other Gospels record only one visit to Jerusalem—the time of Jesus' death. The shorter ministry in the first three Gospels may be a result of a schematization of Jesus' ministry that focuses first on teaching in Galilee and then the death in Jerusalem. So perhaps these other Gospels have squeezed the Temple incident into the only occasion for a Temple visit, given their model of a one-year ministry. But perhaps also John has moved the incident to an early placement to make a theological point. Either way, we are left without a firm idea of when the Temple incident really occurred. But in John's Gospel, the Temple altercation marks the beginning of conflict with the Jewish leadership and thus provides a thematic struggle early in the Gospel that will serve to define the course of the narrative.

The Passover was one of the three holy feasts for which observant Jews were expected to journey to Jerusalem. Passover, Tabernacles, and Weeks (Pentecost) are explicitly mentioned in the Old Testament as feasts to be held in Jerusalem (Leviticus 23), and John's Gospel locates Jesus in Jerusalem for Passover (John 2:13; 6:4; 11:55) and Tabernacles (John 7:10), as well as for the Feast of the Dedication (Hanukkah— John 10:22). It is also possible that he refers to Pentecost (see the reference to "a festival" at John 5:1). So John understands Jesus to be an observant Jew who regularly journeys to Jerusalem for the festivals. This fact alone explains some of the back-and-forth nature of the geographical features of the Gospel.

> "One wonders immediately how much John wishes to say to his contemporaries about men of learning and influence who do not have the courage to profess their faith openly. Nicodemus will be portrayed as a 'teacher of Israel' opaque about fundamentals, which may be his 'night.'"— Sloyan, *John*, Interpretation, 43.

It is unfortunate that this incident has often been called a Temple "cleansing." There is nothing in the incident itself or in the practices that are disrupted to suggest that Jesus saw anything "unclean" taking place. The Temple practices required that a significant number of sacrificial animals be available for slaughter. If pilgrims came from some distance, it was impractical for them to bring animals with them, and they might not always have unblemished animals—a clear requirement of the law. So the sale of animals was necessary for the Temple sacrificial system to be maintained. And the Temple tax was also required, and not in Roman but in Tyrean coinage. It has been suggested that these animals and coins were sold by the Temple priesthood at a high rate of profit, thus implicating them in corrupt practices. But there is nothing in the text that indicates any condemnation of profiteering.

Instead, Jesus' action in the Temple suggests a prophetic act. By tipping over the tables of the money changers and driving out the sellers and their animals, Jesus symbolically disrupted the activity that supported the Temple worship. Moreover, the action of tipping over and driving out seems to point toward the violent destruction of the Temple and the expulsion of the people from its precincts that would take place in the near future. The Fourth Evangelist has Jesus explicitly link his action to the destruction of the Temple. When asked for a sign that will explain why he is performing this action in the Temple (John 2:18), Jesus says, "Destroy this temple, and in three days I will raise it up." "The answer Jesus gives is the sole Johannine prediction of the passion," Sloyan writes (41). The disciples later, after the resurrection, come to understand this as a reference to Jesus' body—which is indeed one of the meanings of the action. The saying becomes another sign that is apprehended after the fact through the eyes of faith. In Christian theology, Jesus' body—the church—does become the new Temple, which is built without hands (cf. Mark 14:58). But the Temple itself was also destroyed in 70 C.E., and so Jesus' sign anticipates his own death *and* the destruction of the Temple.

"The Jews"

It is important for the development of the story that "the Jews" are introduced here and are seen in some conflict with Jesus. As we noted in the Introduction, *the Jews* is a term John's Gospel uses to refer to those in Judaism who actively oppose Jesus and his mission, and it does not refer to all Jews or to the entire nation of Israel.

We might ask, then: Who are these "Jews"? Is John suggesting that the inhabitants of Judea (as the term *the Jews* is often translated) are opposed to Jesus, perhaps in contrast to the inhabitants of Galilee? While this certainly avoids any use of the term *Jews* to label all of Judaism as being opposed to Jesus and therefore implicated in his death, it is hardly supported by the text. Not all Judeans oppose Jesus, and "the Jews" appear even in Galilee. Alternatively, are "the Jews" the religious and cult leaders of the Jewish nation? This would appear to be closer to John's idea, since the term *the Jews* often is closely related to the Pharisees and the chief priests. But even here it is difficult to equate the two. John at times goes to great lengths to use the terms differently, although there is clearly some relationship between them.

> "Clearly not all the Jews were hostile toward Jesus and his followers. It is important, therefore, when we reflect on texts that speak about 'the Jews' to keep this in mind. Especially we should not move from 'the Jews' of Jesus' time to contemporary Jews, thereby continuing the animosity that for too long has poisoned the relationship and distorted understanding between Christians and Jews."—Rhodes, *Mighty Acts of God*, 242.

It is perhaps preferable to see John's term *the Jews* as a designation for those Israelites who oppose Jesus, who actively refuse to consider him the Messiah, and who actively seek to still his voice and his testimony. The term does not relate to any one recognizable geographical or political group, although John understands the religious leaders to be a major component of the opposition to Jesus.

With the action in the Temple, in which the destruction of the Temple is prophetically announced, Jesus begins to develop opponents. These opponents will grow more strident and emphatic in their opposition to Jesus, which is an essential part of the story. "He came to what was his own, and his own people did not accept him" (John 1:10). This opposition in John's Gospel begins early in the ministry of Jesus.

The Dialogue with Nicodemus (3:1–21)

Nicodemus is a character who appears three times in the Fourth Gospel: here, in the first extensive dialogue of the Gospel; again when the Temple police attempt to arrest Jesus (John 7:45–52), and finally at the tomb, after Jesus is dead (John 19:39). One is not sure how to understand Nicodemus. He is, on the one hand, a leading member of the Jewish council and therefore participates in the council that ultimately has Jesus arrested and killed. On the other hand, it appears that he is somewhat open to Jesus, as the dialogue with Jesus and the dispute with the Pharisees seem to indicate. It is too much to call him a secret disciple, but the portrayal of Nicodemus suggests that even leaders of the Jews might have remained somewhat open to Jesus. Perhaps his bringing spices for burial in the final scene implies that Nicodemus belatedly recognized Jesus as Messiah; but the text never comes out and says that. Instead, Nicodemus remains throughout a cryptic figure about whom we are left to ponder and question.

The story of Nicodemus begins with a nighttime visitation. Perhaps this is because he is afraid of the reaction of the other "Jews." Perhaps the night is meant to signify the spiritual darkness in which the Jewish leadership is enveloped. The Fourth Evangelist, in the Prologue, has already interpreted Jesus' coming as one of light coming into darkness, so the use of night here may imply some sense of spiritual constraint. And Jesus' statements to Nicodemus expand on this dark/light metaphor, as if to emphasize the spiritual quality of the cover of night that brings Nicodemus to Jesus:

> And this is the judgment, that the light has come into the world, and people loved darkness rather than light because their deeds were evil. For all who do evil hate the light and do not come to the light, so that their deeds may not be exposed. But those who do what is true come to the light, so that it may be clearly seen that their deeds have been done in God. (3:19–21)

Nicodemus's opening question seems to imply that he is prepared to see Jesus as a special emissary of God; the signs Jesus has performed must come from God. But the resulting dialogue shows instead a miscommunication and failed understanding. In response to Nicodemus's question, Jesus answers that one must be born anew/from above to see the kingdom of God, and Nicodemus misinterprets Jesus' words. Jesus' final statement interprets Nicodemus's misunderstanding as spiritual ignorance and lack of belief. Nicodemus leaves the scene with no final statement of his own, only the implicit condemnation as one who has not received Jesus or his testimony.

The basis for the miscommunication lies in the double meaning of the phrase used for "born again." The Greek adverb *anothen*, which modifies the verb "to be born," has two possible meanings. It can mean "again," as Nicodemus interprets it, or it can mean "from above." The latter meaning is what Jesus suggests (contrary to bumper stickers that claim you cannot enter the kingdom of God "unless you are born again") and serves as

Want to Know More?

About the wedding at Cana? See Carol A. Newsom and Sharon H. Ringe, eds., *Women's Bible Commentary*, expanded ed. (Louisville, Ky.: Westminster John Knox Press, 1998), 383.

About the use of the term the Jews in John? See Robert Kysar, *John: The Maverick Gospel*, rev. ed. (Louisville, Ky.: Westminster John Knox Press, 1993), 67–70.

About Jewish holidays in the New Testament? See *The Access Bible* (New York: Oxford University Press, 1999), 154; Paul J. Achtemeier, ed., *HarperCollins Bible Dictionary*, rev. ed. (New York: HarperCollins, 1998), 334–35.

the basis for his subsequent discussion about being a man from heaven who tells of heavenly things (cf. 3:12–13). He is "from above," and he brings the Spirit that allows others to be born "from above."

In the course of responding to Nicodemus's misunderstanding, Jesus introduces in his own words some of the key theological concepts of the Gospel, concepts that are decisive. Jesus says he has come to bring eternal life to all who believe in him. This statement expands on a theme introduced in the Prologue, that the Word is the author of life. Now Jesus, the Word made flesh, has come to bring that life forever as eternal life.

This theme, the gift of eternal life to those who believe in him, becomes a familiar refrain throughout the rest of the Gospel. And though the concept of believing in Jesus has already been introduced, Jesus' speech emphasizes the crucial importance of belief. Those who believe have eternal life and escape judgment; those who do not believe do not receive eternal life and are condemned already by their actions. The essential and unique nature of Jesus is now made clear. He was identified as the "only begotten" Son in the Prologue. Now that uniqueness is given a functional quality as well—only through belief in this only Son is eternal life bestowed on humanity.

? Questions for Reflection

1. Discuss the exchange between Jesus and his mother. Does this make Jesus appear distant from Mary? Why or why not?

2. The author says it is unfortunate that the Temple incident has been labeled a "cleansing." Do you agree or disagree? If it was not a cleansing, what type of act was it?

3. The author writes that we should not take John's use of the phrase *the Jews* literally to mean all Jewish people or all of Judaism. Can you think of instances today where broad generalizations have been made about a specific group of people? How is this harmful?

4. There has been much speculation about the character and motives of Nicodemus. What do you make of him? What do you think he was after?

3

The Varied Responses to Jesus

After Jesus' dialogue with Nicodemus, the Fourth Evangelist turns again to the witness of John the Baptist. The brief exchange between John the Baptist and his disciples presents an interesting perspective on the relationship between John's ministry and Jesus' ministry and sets the stage for Jesus' return to Galilee—a return that presents a number of diverse responses to Jesus. The second witness of John the Baptist about Jesus' nature serves to round out the beginning of the Gospel—Jesus' initial appearance and call of disciples—and allows a transition to a wider ministry and a more varied revelation of his nature.

Jesus' Baptizing Ministry (3:22–4:3)

According to the Fourth Gospel, Jesus practiced a ministry of baptism in Judea at the same time as John. This simultaneous baptizing ministry is never reported in the Synoptic Gospels, but there is good reason to believe that John is recounting a historical feature from the early period of Jesus' ministry. That Jesus drew some of his disciples from John's disciples and then followed with a similar ministry is very likely.

This similar baptizing ministry could have been a point of confusion between the Baptist's followers and those of Jesus; indeed, the Fourth Gospel is quite willing to entertain that possibility. The Pharisees appear to consider Jesus' ministry to be simply an offshoot of John's, perhaps even a rival ministry, and seek clarification from John about the relationship between the two. This confusion, however, provides one more opportunity to emphasize John the Baptist's subordinate relationship to Jesus. John the Baptist once again testifies that (1) he is not the Messiah and (2) his own ministry must diminish in order to allow Jesus' ministry to grow; both declarations recall his previous words in 1:24–34.

> "Examination of rabbinical sources discloses that human need takes precedence over any prohibition of activity on the sabbath. Since this is the principle Jesus follows in all four Gospels, we must conclude that his followers and those of the rabbis were in constant confrontation after his death over how the principle they held in common was to be applied."—Sloyan, *John*, Interpretation, 80.

John's reputation in Judea undoubtedly was strong and perhaps had some effect on how the early church recounted the traditions of John the Baptist within the narrative about Jesus. The other three Gospels, perhaps because of this strong reputation, tend to tell very little about John's relationship to Jesus other than that he baptized Jesus and then was killed by Herod. The Fourth Gospel's greater interest in the Baptist's relationship to Jesus' ministry necessitates more extensive comments to interpret their relationship. Not only does John testify twice that Jesus is greater, but Jesus also chooses to avoid the controversy such a comparison would cause and instead departs from Judea to Galilee (4:1–3). Moreover, the evangelist, both in Jesus' speech (5:33, 36) and in narrative summaries (10:40–42), informs the reader that while John was a true witness, Jesus' signs and testimony are greater and more valuable, and Jesus more reliably discloses the nature of his own glory.

The Woman of Samaria (4:4–42)

On departing from Judea, Jesus has a dialogue with a Samaritan woman, a story that is unique to John's Gospel. It shows Jesus dealing substantively with a non-Jew in a way that is suggestive of the power of the gospel in the entire Hellenistic world. Furthermore, the exchange works on a play of words, a double meaning similar to that in the Nicodemus incident, in order to explore the life-giving role Jesus plays in the life of the believer. This exchange is very important as it is both christological and evangelistic, thus establishing a framework for subsequent believers.

The narrative begins with Jesus being left alone at the well of Jacob in Samaria. Jesus is met at the well in the middle of the day by a woman from the nearby town, and he asks her to draw some water from the well. In a deprecatory manner, perhaps as a way of expressing disdain for Jesus' Jewishness and certainly touching on the religious and ethnic antipathy that existed between the Jews and the Samaritans, the woman expresses surprise that Jesus would actually ask for water from a Samaritan. The woman, with control over the well, appears to be in control of the situation. Much to the woman's surprise (and the reader's also), Jesus turns this around and suggests that if she only recognized who he was, she would be asking *him* for living water.

> "Jesus is speaking to a Samaritan, symbolic of her people. . . . Jesus knows everything Samaria ever did from a Jewish viewpoint: false worship, consorting with Judah's enemies, whatever the Jews of Judah in the south ever thought the kingdom of Israel in the north was guilty of. Despite this complete knowledge of Jesus about them, the Samaritans are portrayed as a people accepted. Nothing is forgotten but all is forgiven."—Sloyan, *John*, Interpretation, 56.

Jesus' initial response makes use of a double meaning of the term *living water*. It was the usual term for running water, water that flowed from streams or springs and was valued more than water from cisterns or wells. Jewish purification baths (the *miqvah*) were deemed more effective if they contained living water rather than standing water. Jesus' response to the woman suggests that he knows of a spring with living water, which would be superior to the water from Jacob's well. The Samaritan woman's response, "Give me this water," is the expected response, but it shows a failure to appreciate the real issue at stake. While the Samaritan woman understands the term in the normal sense, Jesus seems to be referring metaphorically to water that "gives life," and this is not really water at all but rather some life-giving quality that flows from belief in Jesus himself. The misunderstanding of the term *living water*, then, is comparable to Nicodemus's misunderstanding of the term *born from above/anew*.

When the conversation is derailed by the woman's request for this water, Jesus shifts the focus to the woman's situation. When he asks the woman to return with her husband, she is forced to acknowledge that she has no husband.

> "If you knew the gift of God, and who it is that is saying to you 'Give me a drink,' you would have asked him, and he would have given you living water" (John 4:10).

Jesus demonstrates a miraculous knowledge when he states that she has had five husbands and that the man she lives with now is not her husband. While this could be taken symbolically (some, for instance, see in this a reference to the Samaritans' history), it appears in the narrative to be simply a prophetic understanding of the woman's life situation. And she interprets the statement as such.

At this point the Samaritan woman, though acknowledging the prophetic nature of Jesus' speech, proceeds to test Jesus within the context of the Jewish/Samaritan distinction. The deep antipathy between Jews and Samaritans prevents the woman from accepting Jesus simply on the basis of the "sign" given by his special knowledge of her situation. Instead, the woman asks a provocative question about the worship practices of the Samaritans. It is as if she is challenging Jesus to denounce the Samaritan worship, and Samaritans as well, thus confirming her suspicion of him as a Jew who "writes off" the Samaritans as religiously improper outsiders.

While Jesus does assert that the Samaritan worship practices are in error, he contextualizes this statement first by saying that both Jewish and Samaritan worship practices are transitory and will be superceded by worship "in spirit and truth." This understanding of an end-time worship levels the ground between Samaritan and Jew and leaves open the complete reconciliation of the two groups. Jesus is, in effect, embracing the Samaritans as worthy of God's attention and able to approach God in the worship that will come. So, rather than accentuate the differences between the Samaritans and the Jews, Jesus reaches out to include the Samaritans in a new view of "kingdom."

The woman, drawing on Jesus' statement that "the hour is coming," apparently interprets this prediction messianically. Her response acknowledges that the Samaritans also look forward to a messianic age and to the expectation of a messiah who will prophetically reveal the will of God. In this the woman was echoing the expectation of the Samaritans for Ta'eb, the messiah who was predicted by Moses in Deuteronomy 18:18. But in seeing this only as a future possibility ("I know that Messiah is coming. . . . When he comes . . ."), she has missed Jesus' strong statement of present fulfillment: "The hour is coming, and is now here." There remains a chasm of misunderstanding between the woman and Jesus.

Jesus concludes the exchange, then, with a bold revelation of his own nature. "I am he, the one who is speaking to you." In the Greek, the sentence is not unambiguously a revelation of Jesus' nature as the Christ. It could simply say, "I am the one speaking to you," which is an odd statement at the conclusion of an extended conversation. But in this statement Jesus first uses the phrase "I am" (Greek, *ego eimi*), which will be repeated in a number of variations later in the Gospel, almost always with some emphatic christological context: "*I am* the light of the world"; "*I am* the bread that comes down from heaven"; "before Abraham was, *I am.*" Moreover, the only previous use of this term is John the Baptist's negative use: "*I am not* the Christ" (John 1:20; 3:28). It appears to be a form of self-revelation, although it is still cloaked in ambiguity and allows for possible misinterpretation.

But the woman does not, in fact, misinterpret Jesus' assertion about his own nature. Perhaps the accumulation of prophetic speech and self-assertion was particularly powerful. At any rate, the woman immediately returns to her village to tell of her encounter and to suggest that Jesus may be the Messiah. She phrases the question to leave open the possibility that such a conclusion is wrong; the NRSV has accurately captured the hesitancy in the question, "He cannot be the Messiah, can he?" The woman is only tentatively a believer in Jesus. But because of her statement, the Samaritans invite Jesus to stay with them, and many come to believe independent of her witness. The exchange between Jesus and the Samaritan woman bears fruit in many Samaritans' belief in Jesus' identity as the savior of the world. In this context, the word *world* is crucially important, for Jesus has shown that God's plan extends beyond the narrow confines of Judaism even to the Samaritans, and by extension, to the Gentiles.

> "[Jesus] breaks open boundaries in his conversation with the Samaritan woman: the boundary between male and female, the boundary between 'chosen people' and 'rejected people.' Jesus' journey to Samaria and his conversation with the woman demonstrate that the grace of God that he offers is available to all."—Gail O'Day, in Newsom and Ringe, eds., *Women's Bible Commentary*, 384.

Healing of the Official's Son (4:43–54)

After the exchange with the Samaritans, the Fourth Gospel relates a healing story that bears a strong similarity to one found in Matthew and Luke: the healing of an official's son. This story appears to serve a number of purposes in John's narrative construction. It provides another "sign" of Jesus' nature, and it demonstrates a positive response of faith to this revelation of his nature. Furthermore, it structurally relates this healing to the wedding at Cana, Jesus' first sign, thus providing a sense of unity to Jesus' actions. Two significant markers indicate this structural linkage in John's narrative. First, the healing story is introduced by a backward glance to the first sign, the wedding at Cana, by means of two explicit references—to Cana as the location of the present action and to Jesus' previous sign at Cana, that of changing water to wine. Second, the incident closes with a comment that this was the *second* sign Jesus performed after coming to Galilee. It appears that the Fourth Evangelist wants to highlight this healing in a particular way.

But before dealing with the Fourth Gospel's account of the healing of the official's son or the problems related to understanding its perspective on faith and signs, we must first deal with the interpretation of Jesus' return to Galilee. John emphatically draws attention to the geographical location by means of anticipatory statements that frame the events that follow. But this geographical reference creates an interesting difficulty of its own.

> "Then Jesus said to them, 'Prophets are not without honor, except in their hometown, and among their own kin, and in their own house'" (Mark 6:4).

According to John's Gospel, Jesus leaves Samaria for Galilee "because a prophet has no honor in the prophet's own country" (4:44). This explanation bristles with problems. Is Jesus leaving Samaria because it (Samaria) is not honoring him? This is the least likely explanation, since it is almost impossible that John understood Samaria as Jesus' homeland. Besides, the narrative describes this village in Samaria as believing in him. Alternatively, is this statement an extension of Jesus leaving Judea (referring back to 4:3)? If so, then John is suggesting that Jesus' homeland is Judea. While this agrees with the general pattern that opposition to Jesus has occurred and will continue to occur in Judea, and especially in Jerusalem, elsewhere in the Fourth Gospel, Jesus is always linked to Galilee (see 1:45; 6:42; 7:41, 52; 18:5, 7; 19:19). So it is unlikely that the Fourth Evangelist wanted to assert that Jesus originated in Judea. But the idea that Jesus goes to Galilee to encounter problems is contrary to the narrative: not only is his reception in Galilee generally better than that in Judea, but in this particular account, Jesus is immediately welcomed by Galileans upon his arrival (John 4:45), which invalidates the prophetic statement.

This leaves two possibilities: either Jesus' statement about his "country" is meant to be a statement not about origins but rather about a spiritual or intentional relationship or it is meant to be ironic. I take it that both interpretations are correct. While the Fourth Gospel acknowledges throughout that Jesus comes from Galilee, he also comes to "his own," which must mean the people of Israel, symbolically linked especially to Jerusalem and the Temple. No other

34

Gospel has such an interest in Jerusalem. And in the narrative immediately preceding, the exchange with the woman from Samaria, Jesus refers to the Jews and the Jerusalem cult as the present locus of appropriate worship and source of salvation. The transition paragraph of 4:43–45, then, serves to create a sense of Jesus' "spiritual" homeland; and this "true" homeland is, ironically, the one that rejects Jesus most emphatically. In contrast, his actual homeland, Galilee, accepts him readily, and his signs produce belief there.

The account of the healing is fairly straightforward. A royal official's son is dying in Capernaum. The royal official begs Jesus for healing. After a statement that could be taken as a rebuff or as an encouragement, the official asks again, and Jesus declares that the son will live. The official returns home to find the son well and subsequently responds with faith. It is very similar to the accounts in Luke and Matthew. A significant difference from the Synoptic accounts, however, is the identification of this man as a royal official (most likely a member of the court of Herod Antipas) and the sick person as his son. The identification of the man as a royal official on Herod's court might mean he was technically a Jew (as opposed to the clearly Gentile centurion in Matthew and Luke). The other significant difference is Jesus' initial response: "Unless you see signs and wonders you will not believe" (John 4:48).

A key question in understanding John's account is whether Jesus' statement to the royal official is meant as a negative or a positive assessment of signs. It is common in Johannine scholarship to view this as a negative statement, that is, that Jesus is perturbed at the request for healing because faith engendered in this fashion is somehow inferior to faith that springs unaided by signs. But such a view, in my opinion, reads too much into the text at this point. Jesus simply states that signs and wonders can, in fact, be useful for bringing about faith. The result is that the royal official initially believes Jesus' words and then responds, along with his whole household, with an expression of belief. While the final response is not entirely clear—it never explicitly says that the official and his household believed in Jesus as Messiah—it seems apparent that this is the import of the statement and the thrust of the whole passage. Jesus performs a sign, and the man and his household believe. Structurally, this is parallel to the first sign at Cana, where Jesus performed a sign and the disciples believed in him. The narrator's comment that this was the second sign, which draws our memory back to the first sign, suggests the evangelist wants the reader to consider that parallel.

While it might be inappropriate to base too much on one account, the account of the royal official's son's healing offers little basis to believe that the Fourth Gospel has a negative view of signs as leading to faith; nor is there any indication that such faith is of a lower order than faith derived from simply hearing Jesus. Signs are part of how Jesus reveals his glory. Granted, the signs might be misinterpreted or ignored, and Jesus seems to find it necessary to interpret himself to his audience. But signs and testimony are both validated by the Fourth Evangelist as ways to perceive Jesus for who he is—the creative Word of God.

Healing on the Sabbath (5:1–18)

In what is beginning to take shape as a pattern for John's Gospel, Jesus immediately returns to Jerusalem, this time on the occasion of an unnamed "festival of the Jews." If we seek to construct a chronological timeline, which might not be crucial to John's purpose in the Gospel, we may interpret this festival as being Pentecost, or Weeks, celebrated in the late spring. A previous trip to Jerusalem had been at the festival of Passover (chapter 2), and a subsequent trip (chapter 7) will be in the autumn at the feast of Tabernacles. Pentecost, Passover, and Tabernacles are the three major festivals for Judaism, and the Bible contains strong statements about the need to celebrate them in Jerusalem (see Deut. 16:16; on the festival of Pentecost, see Lev. 23:15–22; Num. 28:26–31; Deut. 16:9–12). However, chapter 6 of John is placed near Passover (6:4), which is in early spring, before Pentecost, so the unnamed festival might be Tabernacles. Or perhaps, as Sloyan states in his *Interpretation* commentary, there has been some displacement in the text, or the author has many accounts and makes no attempt to place them in an absolute chronological order. What is important is that Jesus returns to Jerusalem, and his trips tend to coincide with festivals.

Once again, the Fourth Evangelist relates a miraculous sign. This time it is the healing of a paralytic who seeks a cure at the Sheep Pool. Jesus, after inquiring whether the man wants to be healed, commands him to pick up his mat and walk. Jesus' command here is almost identical to the healing of the paralytic in the Synoptic tradition (Mark 2:11; cf. Matt. 9:7; Luke 5:24), although the setting and circumstances are completely different.

The focus of the story, however, is not on the healing itself but rather on the controversy that follows. Since the healing was on the

Sabbath, "the Jews" accuse Jesus of doing work on the Sabbath. In response, Jesus offers his defense: "My Father is still working, and I also am working" (5:17). This response serves only to harden "the Jews" in their opposition to Jesus, such that they seek to kill Jesus. The basis for their opposition is summarized by John in a three-fold argument:

> Jesus was breaking the Sabbath.
>
> Jesus was calling God his own Father.
>
> Thus, Jesus was making himself equal to God.

It is easy, of course, to dismiss the Jewish opposition to Jesus as blind and narrow. But protection of the Sabbath is a duty under the law given by God and is crucial for protecting the holiness of God among God's people. Sabbath breaking is a serious offense. But more serious would be any attempt by a Jew to deny its requirement. By claiming to be able to work on the Sabbath because God is also working, Jesus in fact claims a special exemption by virtue of his relationship with God. "The Jews," then, are quite correct in deducing that Jesus claims equality with God, or at least a special filial relationship.

The Fourth Evangelist allows the Jews to make a number of true statements about Jesus that, ironically, place them in

Want to Know More?

About different understandings of baptism? See Alan Richardson and John Bowden, *The Westminster Dictionary of Christian Theology* (Philadelphia: Westminster Press, 1983), 299–302; J. G. Davies, ed., *The Westminster Dictionary of Liturgy and Worship* (Philadelphia: Westminster Press, 1986), 55–77.

About John the Baptist? See Paul J. Achtemeier, ed., *HarperCollins Bible Dictionary*, rev. ed. (New York: HarperCollins, 1996), 538–39.

About the portrayal of women in the Bible? See Carol A. Newsom and Sharon H. Ringe, eds., *Women's Bible Commentary*, expanded ed. (Louisville, Ky.: Westminster John Knox Press, 1998), 251–59, 482–88. For a more technical treatment, see Gail Corrington Streete, *The Strange Woman: Power and Sex in the Bible* (Louisville, Ky.: Westminster John Knox Press, 1997); for an excellent, very readable treatment, see Frank Stagg and Evelyn Stagg, *Woman in the World of Jesus* (Philadelphia: Westminster Press, 1978).

About healing? See Donald K. McKim, *Encyclopedia of the Reformed Faith* (Louisville, Ky.: Westminster John Knox Press, 1992), 164–65; Zach Thomas, *Healing Touch: The Church's Forgotten Language* (Louisville, Ky.: Westminster John Knox Press, 1994).

complete opposition to him. In this they betray their darkness and their opposition to God as well. It is not that they do not make the right deductions from Jesus' statement but rather that they do not recognize Jesus for who he really is. Thus the development of the opposition to Jesus that was first broached in the Prologue ("He came to what was his own, and his own people did not accept him") is based on darkness and not ignorance. "The Jews'" opposition grows not from lack of knowledge but from a lack of light and a lack of desire to accept the Son of God.

The Authority of the Witnesses to Jesus (5:19–47)

In response to the opposition of "the Jews," Jesus defends himself in a monologue. There is no response to Jesus' monologue, and it must be presumed that his speech is more of a literary artifice than a real dialogue with the Jewish opposition. No one in the story appears to have been convinced, for the opposition to Jesus only grows, and there is no report of anyone believing in Jesus based on this speech. But at the same time, the absence of a retort to Jesus' monologue suggests a completeness and, indeed, a satisfactory rebuttal to the opposition's charges, for the opposition is left speechless—in fact if not in thought.

Jesus' response to the opposition rests on three bold claims, based on a full approval of the charge that Jesus calls himself God's Son:

1. The Son is sent from the Father, and thus his work is directly related to the Father's work and receives its authority and power from God.
2. The Son has received the authority to execute judgment.
3. There is ample testimony to who Jesus is, and the failure to acknowledge that reality is not a failure of information but a spiritual failure.

The first of these propositions serves, in part, to defend Jesus against the misapprehension that he is working in some way independent of or at odds with God. Underlying the Jewish charge against him—that he claims to be equal with God—is the supposition that he is therefore independent of or in competition with the one God of the Israelites. Jesus is at great pains, then, to argue that he is subordinate to God. But at the same time he proposes that he functions as God's designated agent. God's activities are indeed being made manifest through the activities of Jesus. This argument both blunts the possible offense of "claiming equality" and establishes a claim that turns the accusation back against "the Jews." If Jesus is acting in God's stead, as God's agent, then opposition to Jesus is opposition to God. "Anyone who does not honor the Son does not honor the Father who sent him" (5:23).

The second proposition is perhaps bolder still, that is, that the Son has been given the power of judgment. Judgment is the prerogative of God, an idea Jesus affirms by saying that the activity of judging has been given by the Father to the Son (5:22). This judgment is the power over life itself. And yet Jesus' judgment is never disconnected from God; it merely expresses God's will (5:30).

An intriguing element of Jesus' monologue is the presence of overlapping ideas of present judgment and future judgment. His role as judge is understood as related to his role as the "Son of Man." In keeping with similar statements in the other Gospels, the title "Son of Man" is frequently connected to a future event in which the world comes to an end and is finally judged. This is perhaps most clearly seen in Mark 13:24–27, where Jesus has linked a prophecy from Isaiah 34 with a statement from Daniel 7 to announce a dramatic expectation: the conclusion of the great drama will see the Son of Man descending from heaven in power to execute judgment in favor of the elect. The same idea is echoed in the Fourth Gospel's version of Jesus' speech. As the Son of Man, Jesus executes judgment, even extending to that time when all will rise from the graves, some to life and some to condemnation (John 5:27–29). At the same time, however, the Fourth Evangelist understands that judgment is a present reality. Those who accept Jesus and honor him as coming from the Father have already been judged favorably and have received life (John 5:24, 25). While judgment is indeed a reality of the end times—the eschaton—it manifests itself immediately and can thus be said to have already taken place.

The third proposition rests on the legal nature of this speech. Jesus defends himself against charges that he is blasphemous because he equates himself with God. In a trial, it is common to call witnesses for the defense. Jesus does just that by calling on three kinds of witnesses that support his character. First, he recalls the testimony of John the Baptist, who was acknowledged as upright and prophetic. But such testimony, Jesus says, is only partial. So he adds a second testimony, that of the very works God has given Jesus to do. Signs were often used as evidence in antiquity, and in this case Jesus says that the

---

Jesus Responds

Jesus' response to the opposition rests on three bold claims:

1. The Son is sent from the Father, and his work receives its authority and power from God.
2. The Son has received the authority to execute judgment.
3. There is ample testimony to who Jesus is; the failure to acknowledge that reality is not a failure of information but a spiritual failure.

signs are God's own testimony on behalf of Jesus (5:37). Specifically, the signs Jesus has performed are testimony that Jesus acts on God's behalf. And finally, Jesus calls on the testimony of ancient witnesses—the scriptures. In so doing, Jesus actually calls Moses as a witness against the prosecution. The activity of God among the Israelites has laid the groundwork for Jesus, and thus the failure to perceive Jesus as acting in accord with the ancient witnesses is a failure to acknowledge God's ancient testimony. By invoking Moses against Jesus, "the Jews" actually admit their own spiritual darkness.

As in the previous dialogue with Nicodemus, Jesus responds to both question and accusation with a strong support of his ministry. As his ministry and activity unfold, he increasingly meets opposition from the Jewish leadership. Although "the Jews" respond with silence to his argument, they give neither acceptance nor statement of belief. The drama of opposition to Jesus is just beginning.

? Questions for Reflection

1. Who are the Samaritans in our society? Does your church attempt to "meet them at the well"? What can Jesus' words to the Samaritan woman say to us, living in a pluralistic world?
2. Talk about John 4:48. Is this a negative or positive assessment of signs? What might Jesus have meant?
3. Why did "the Jews" want to kill Jesus (5:18)? What did they use for justification?
4. Read the three points of Jesus' response to the opposition (John 5:19–47), summarized on page 38 of this study. The Jewish leaders did not respond to his arguments here, but if they had, what do you think their response would have been?

4

Jesus Himself as Sign

After the accusation of blasphemy by "the Jews" in Jerusalem, Jesus returns to Galilee to continue his ministry. But the die has been cast. The Jewish leadership are hardening their stance against him, and Jesus is becoming increasingly open in displaying his mission and ministry to those who will listen. The opportunity for Jesus' audience to perceive who he is, and thus also to believe, widens as he openly explains his mission. He reveals that he not only performs signs but indeed himself functions as a sign of God's life-giving activity among humanity. But, paradoxically, this open demonstration of his purpose also demands a response—a response that is not always positive.

Feeding of the Five Thousand and Walking on the Water (6:1–24)

John's report of the miraculous feeding of five thousand (6:1–15) is remarkably similar to that found in the other Gospels. Indeed, this miracle is the only one that is closely similar in all the Gospels. The essential elements are all here. Jesus goes with his disciples to a remote location, and a large crowd numbering five thousand follows them. With concern over their lack of food, Jesus takes five loaves of bread and two fish and, after blessing them, distributes them to the crowd. The food is sufficient to satisfy the people, and the disciples are able to collect twelve baskets of fragments left over from the food.

John places this miracle close to the Passover, which is the second Passover mentioned in the Gospel. This event, then, is either approximately six or ten months later than the festival noted in chapter 5, depending on whether that unnamed festival was Tabernacles or Pentecost. Either way, the lapse of time is significant. But the notation of the Passover time reminds us again that John is very aware of the Jewish festival seasons, and it may also suggest a connection between the feeding in the wilderness and the Feast of Unleavened Bread, which is closely connected with Passover. Since the Passover is also related to the exodus from Egypt, during which time the Israelites subsisted on manna, we should not be surprised that the theme of bread and manna would be expanded on in the dialogue that follows.

Perhaps an equally important variation in the Johannine account of the miraculous feeding, however, is the conclusion of the initial miracle. Here the crowd understands the miracle to be a sign, in keeping with John's perspective that these are signs of some reality not readily apparent. For the crowd, the miracle is a sign that Jesus is a prophet and a king. The crowd echoes the language of Deuteronomy 18:15–18, where Moses predicts a future prophet will come who will be like Moses himself: "The Lord your God will raise up for you a prophet like me from among your own people." Key to this understanding is the phrase "a prophet like me": this was interpreted to be a specific individual to come, not just any prophetic figure. At the same time, however, there is some reason to see a reference to Elijah here, not Moses. "The one who is to come into the world" at John 6:14 is suggestive of Elijah (see Mal. 4:5 for this expectation). And it is intriguing that Elisha, Elijah's successor, also multiplied barley loaves for a miraculous feeding (2 Kgs. 4:42).

> "Jesus knows what the true bread from heaven is. It is neither the manna of old nor the miraculously multiplied food of the previous day. The crowd does not say 'What is it?'. . . . but, 'We want it.' Knowing what you want out of life is half the battle, if you want the right things."—Sloyan, *John,* Interpretation, 69.

But the crowd also wants to make Jesus a king. In this they are drawing on messianic ideas, primarily the idea that one like David would come and would be king of Israel. There is some evidence in Judaism, particularly from the group who produced the Dead Sea Scrolls, that messianic expectation drew on expectations for a prophet to come before the messiah. The Mosaic "prophet-like-me" expectation could well have been conflated with the Elijah expectation and linked as well with the "Davidic/kingly" expectation. It is frankly unclear what the people were expecting—they may well have had a variety of conceptions that were not neatly separated.

It is also of interest that the very concepts alluded to in the crowd's response have been foreshadowed in the priests' examination of John the Baptist (1:19–21). There the priests ask John if he is (1) the messiah, (2) Elijah, or (3) the prophet; the last term must be a reference to the "prophet-like-me" reference in Deuteronomy 18:15–18. John the Baptist denies each of these roles. These are three different expected individuals, and yet the crowd seems to see in Jesus all three merged together. And perhaps that is the essential point—that Jesus is the culmination of all the prophetic expectations of God's intervention in human affairs.

Just as John's feeding miracle is similar to the accounts in the other Gospels, so also is the Fourth Gospel's report of Jesus walking on the water, found also in Mark and Matthew:

1. The disciples depart in boats without Jesus.
2. A storm arises with strong winds.
3. Jesus, walking on the sea, comes to the boat in which the disciples are struggling.
4. The disciples are afraid.
5. Jesus identifies himself ("It is I") and tells the disciples not to fear.
6. There is a sudden conclusion to the incident.

Jesus' miracles

What is striking in John's account is the lack of a concluding reaction on the part of the disciples. In Matthew, the disciples worship Jesus and call him the Son of God. In Mark, while lacking understanding, the disciples are astounded at the incident. But John's report simply has the disciples glad to take Jesus into the boat. The walking on the water, then, is not recognized by the Fourth Evangelist as a sign, and little is made of it. Instead, it is subsumed into the larger discussion about the feeding miracle, for Jesus' subsequent discourse returns to the subject. It is the feeding that serves as the primary sign of who Jesus is. More meaning is yet to be

> "Kingship for the crowd is national liberation at the hands of a powerful messiah-figure. For John it is the solitary condition of Jesus, the ruler of the end-time (cf. 18:37), as he communes with God on the mountain to which he has withdrawn (v. 15)."—Sloyan, *John*, Interpretation, 65.

discerned in this sign; a simple miraculous event, in contrast, does not by itself signify the nature of Jesus' relationship with God.

Bread from Heaven (6:22–59)

With the disciples' departure and Jesus' subsequent walking on the water, the scene shifts to the other side of the sea, near Capernaum. The crowd has not departed because they did not see Jesus leave in the boat. Thus the narrative link pays attention to the circumstances surrounding the walking on the water, even though the crowd is portrayed as unaware of it. But once the crowd is aware of his absence, they also depart in boats to Capernaum.

What Did People Expect from a Messiah?

In the time of Jesus, there was a complex understanding about who the messiah would be and what he would do. Two strands of thought dominated. The first was that the messiah would be a descendant of David and would rule brilliantly over a new Israel in a blessed era of peace. The second was more in line with the reference in Daniel to a Son of Man, an otherworldly being who coexisted with God and would return at the end of the age to pass judgment. The concept of a messiah who would suffer was completely unknown to the contemporaries of Jesus.

The mysterious departure of Jesus gives rise to the initial question by the crowd: "Rabbi, when did you come here?" (6:25). But Jesus deflects this and instead questions their motives. His response, that they seek him because they were filled by the feeding rather than because they saw signs, is potentially illuminating for an understanding of the signs in the Fourth Gospel. Jesus seems to be making a distinction between the miraculous aspect of a sign (sufficient food to eat) and the spiritual aspect of a sign (the feeding pointing to the real nature of Jesus). It is the latter issue—the spiritual reality of the sign— that will be the focus of Jesus' subsequent discourse.

But at the same time that the distinction between "sign as miracle" and "sign as disclosing a spiritual reality" is intended, there is also a real difficulty in the narrative at this point. We should recall that the concluding scene of the feeding miracle (6:14) has the crowd seeing the miracle as a sign that Jesus is the prophet-king predicted in scripture. While the crowd's conclusion was shown to be in error, it was still a recognition of the act's sign value. Here, in the opening scene on the other side of the shore, Jesus says the crowd was disinterested in signs, only wanting to be fed. This could be an indication of a literary seam or a variant tradition. But perhaps it is just John's way of further criticizing the crowd's reaction to Jesus. The recognition of Jesus as prophet-king is, in John's understanding, fundamentally a self-centered and spiritually deficient understanding.

Jesus exhorts the crowd to work for food that leads to eternal life, but the crowd misunderstands the point and asks instead how they might perform the works of God. It appears that they hear Jesus saying that they, too, can produce this imperishable food, which would make them miracle workers also. They seize on the verb *to work* and are anxious to know how to involve themselves in this activity. But they do not choose to hear the second half of Jesus' exhortation: that this food will be given to them by the Son of Man. In response to their failure properly to understand the nature of "doing work," Jesus simply says that the one work necessary is to believe in him who is sent by God, that is, Jesus. This misunderstanding by the crowd prompts a further request for a validating sign, and in requesting the second sign, the crowd follow a pattern already seen in the Temple incident: Jesus performs a sign; the people ("Jews" in 2:18; the crowd in 6:30) are not ready to trust Jesus and seek further validation.

That the crowd in John 6 was still imagining Jesus as the prophet-like-Moses is seen in their request for a second sign. They cite the miracle of the manna from Exodus 16, presumably to suggest that Moses gave the sign of manna. In other words, they confirm by their own words Jesus' perception of their motives: they want more food, even that which perishes (as the manna did each day). Jesus is to show that he is sent by God by performing the miracle of Moses. In requesting this sign or something like it, the crowd show they misunderstand Jesus' exhortation for them to do works resulting in imperishable food. When Jesus goes on to say that God gives a superior bread from heaven (one giving life), the crowd calls out for this bread. But are they still misunderstanding? Are they not still expecting something like manna, life-giving bread from heaven?

This misunderstanding of the nature of Jesus' feeding miracle and his overall mission establishes the framework for the discourse to follow. Jesus clarifies exactly what this bread from heaven is:

"Then the LORD replied to me: 'They are right in what they have said. I will raise up for them a prophet like you from among their own people; I will put my words in the mouth of the prophet, who shall speak to them everything that I command. Anyone who does not heed the words that the prophet shall speak in my name, I myself will hold accountable'" (Deut. 18:17–18).

"I am the bread of life" (6:35). Jesus himself has come from heaven to give life to those who believe. In this he dispels "spiritual hunger" and "spiritual thirst." The theme that begins in 6:29—that the work that results in eternal food is belief in the one God sent—is now made clear. Those who believe in Jesus as the bread of life will have eternal life, and Jesus will raise them up on the last day (6:40).

The theme of Jesus as life-giving food is developed in two distinct ways. The first emphasizes Jesus as the bread from heaven—a fulfillment of the manna motif. This theme is what we find in 6:35–40 and 6:43–51: Jesus interprets himself as the one sent from heaven, true life-giving bread. But the Fourth Gospel further develops the theme in eucharistic language in 6:53–58. In this discourse, Jesus uses language that appears to anticipate the Lord's Supper. Although, in the first discourse (6:35–51), Jesus finally does suggest that the bread of heaven is his flesh ("I am the living bread that came down from heaven. Whoever eats of this bread will live forever; and the bread that I will give for the life of the world is my flesh"—6:51), the overall thrust of the discourse is a metaphorical bread. But in the latter discourse, Jesus shifts the metaphor more explicitly to his flesh and blood, which is a clearly eucharistic turn. Not only is the metaphor more explicit, but the command is more urgent and essential: "unless you eat the flesh of the Son of Man and drink his blood, you have no life in you" (6:53). It is, of course, intriguing that the Fourth Gospel does not use eucharistic language in its depiction of the Last Supper (13:1–30). But the motif is not absent from John's Gospel, and in this discourse following the feeding miracle is imagery that is equally sacramental in nature.

The Responses to Jesus (6:60–71)

It is not surprising that Jesus' audiences react to this strong metaphorical language. With it Jesus claims to be one (1) who has descended from heaven, (2) who must be the object of the people's belief, and (3) who must be feasted upon in order for them to receive life. As one might expect, "the Jews" react immediately. They see Jesus as the son of Joseph, and as such, he cannot be the one who came from heaven. When Jesus expands the metaphor to refer to his own flesh, "the Jews" react again. It is only surprising that there is no mention at this point of an attempt to kill him, as has occurred already in 5:18.

Perhaps the failure to focus on "the Jews'" reaction is due to John's emphasis at this juncture on Jesus' followers, not on his opponents; for, in response to these hard words, some of Jesus' own disciples draw back from following him. First they question the saying (6:60), and then they withdraw (6:66). The reason for their turning back is stated clearly—they did not believe (6:64).

Such a negative response, however, also allows the Twelve to assert their own belief in Jesus. In response to a question posed by Jesus, Peter speaks for all of them by making an explicit confession of faith: "You have the words of eternal life. We have come to believe and know that you are the Holy One of God" (6:68–69). Yet even here there is a dark shadow, for the first intimation of Judas as betrayer is made. Indeed, he is called a devil, which anticipates the author's later description that the devil enters Judas and leads him to his act of betrayal (13:2, 27).

> **The Miracles of Jesus**
>
> Miracles are recorded in all four Gospels. The overall count is usually given at thirty-seven. Of these, eighteen are found in only one Gospel, six in two Gospels, twelve in three Gospels, and one in four Gospels. The order of the Gospels according to the number of miracles included is as follows: Luke, twenty-two; Matthew, twenty-one; Mark, nineteen; John, eight. See Rhodes, *Mighty Acts of God*, 274.

A final group is portrayed as reacting to Jesus at this point, although it is not directly connected to the feeding miracle. In introducing the next narrative unit, the exchanges in Jerusalem during the Tabernacles feast, the Fourth Evangelist tells us that Jesus' own brothers do not believe in him. Their encouragement for Jesus to go to Judea and openly display his works is seen as a cynical response given from a perspective of disbelief.

The feeding miracle and Jesus' use of the sign to interpret himself to the crowds, then, have resulted in varying responses to Jesus. The degree to which Jesus discloses himself and his relationship to God is the degree to which he demands a response from those around him, and a response, either positive or negative, is given.

The Tabernacles Controversies (7:1–52)

Although Jesus indicated to his brothers that he would not go up to Jerusalem during the Tabernacles feast (7:6–8), he nonetheless does go to Jerusalem. And though John reports that Jesus went up to the city in private because "the Jews" were speaking against him, in the middle of the feast Jesus goes publicly into the Temple to teach. It is in the context of the Tabernacles feast, then, that Jesus makes public proclamations that prompt responses by both "the Jews" and the crowds in Jerusalem. The controversies that take place at Tabernacles are notable because (1) Jesus' proclamations are, in many ways, based on imagery drawn from the Tabernacles practices; (2) there is a clear distinction drawn between "the Jews" and the rest of the Jewish participants in the feast; and (3) the controversies serve to force a reaction, a crisis of decision, on the hearers.

The first controversy begins with Jesus "baiting" his opponents. Referring back to the healing of the man at the Sheep Pool (5:1–18), Jesus asks why "the Jews" were seeking to kill him. If their opposition is based on the Mosaic law (Sabbath observance), then for them to have proper authority to prosecute Jesus, they should at least keep the law themselves. Jesus tacitly accuses the Jews of breaking the law by their very opposition to healing on the Sabbath. Comparing his work with the practice of circumcising on the Sabbath, Jesus claims that healing is well within the law.

> "Do you believe that Jesus lived the only life wholly committed to the will of God? Do you believe that he died for you and that he was raised from the dead? Do you believe in the transformation of life by the Spirit of God? Do you believe in direct revelatory answer to prayer? If you do, you believe in miracle. But more than that, if you are a new creation in Christ, you are a miracle. Biblical faith is miraculous faith. The Bible, the church, and the Christian life cannot be accounted for apart from the mighty acts of God that center in Jesus Christ."—Rhodes, *Mighty Acts of God*, 279.

This return to the Sabbath healing controversy prompts a split reaction. On the one hand, a number of the people believe in Jesus, perhaps impressed that he is able publicly to continue speaking despite the efforts by the leaders to kill him. On the other hand, the Pharisees and chief priests respond by sending officers to arrest Jesus (7:32), a danger that continues to hang over his head throughout the festival.

Some days later, on the last day of the feast, Jesus continues to teach publicly, this time saying that the believer will receive living water that will quench thirst (6:37). In many ways this is reminiscent of Jesus' teaching to the Samaritan woman (cf. 4:10–15), although here the narrator interprets it as the gift of the Holy Spirit that would be given following Jesus' death and resurrection (his "glorification," to use John's term). The introduction of this theme at this point in the story is made clear when one understands some of the activities at the Tabernacles feast. Each day of Tabernacles, water was drawn from the pool of Siloam and carried in golden flasks to the altar, where it was poured out. Jesus employs this imagery of the drawn water to compare to the gift of the Spirit, which will not be drawn or still water but rather living water—which in this case could mean either flowing water or water that itself is full of life. It is quite likely that Jesus is also evoking the prophecy of Zechariah (14:8) that refers to the coming of the messianic end times, with its description of living waters flowing out from the altar itself and watering all the region of Israel. Zechariah also refers to Tabernacles in this context (14:16), so the connection may have been particularly striking to participants at the Tabernacles festival.

> "Let anyone among you who is without sin be the first to throw a stone at her" (John 8:7).

As with the first teaching, Jesus' pronouncement prompts a response. Some of those listening think he is the prophet (see the discussion of the feeding of the five thousand); some think he is the Christ; and others refuse to believe him to be anything special because he came from Galilee. Some of those disbelieving in Jesus want to arrest him. But the result is still no arrest or action against Jesus. The officers sent to arrest Jesus return to the leaders without him because they are amazed at his teaching. In the response that follows, it is clear that the "authorities and Pharisees" are steadfast in opposing Jesus, whereas some from the crowds believe. While Nicodemus continues to be a possible exception to the attitude of the leaders—he requests a trial before Jesus is arrested—in general, the leaders of the Jews maintain a clear opposition to Jesus.

The third controversy takes place after the story of the adulterous woman. Jesus continues his self-disclosure by claiming to be the light of the world. As with the "living waters" metaphor, the "light" metaphor connects with the Tabernacles festival activities. Each night during Tabernacles, large oil candle lights were set up, using the priest's linen garments for the wicks. According to the Mishnah, these candle lights were so bright that "there was not a courtyard in Jerusalem that did not reflect the light of the Beth ha-She'ubah" (*Mishnah Sukkah* 5.3). Presumably, then, Jesus speaks this saying in the evening, when the lights are lit and provide a context for his saying.

> "And Jesus said, 'Neither do I condemn you. Go your way, and from now on do not sin again'" (John 8:11).

As with the previous discourses in the Tabernacles feast, this saying elicits a disagreement and a varying response. The Pharisees criticize Jesus for using this metaphor to refer to himself. In response, Jesus validates his witness by claiming that he alone knows from where he comes and where he is going, and that the true testimony is from God the Father, who bears witness to Jesus. The reference to "where he is going" produces a misunderstanding in some (8:27), yet many believed in him (8:30).

The series of exchanges and teachings in Jerusalem at the Tabernacles feast shows Jesus using a variety of metaphors and images to reveal his nature to the Jewish festivalgoers. Each of the teachings invites a response. In a pattern becoming increasingly clear, the Jewish leaders (sometimes Pharisees, sometimes Pharisees with the chief priests, sometimes simply "the Jews") reject his disclosure and misunderstand his messages. But at each occurrence, among those listening are a number who believe. It is clear, then, that the Jewish people are not inherently opposed to Jesus; belief certainly is possible. But the lines of conflict are hardening, and the choice between belief and disbelief is becoming more tangible with each dialogue and exchange.

The Adulterous Woman (7:53–8:11)

There are notorious textual problems with the Fourth Gospel's account of Jesus and the adulterous woman in John 7:53–8:11. The earliest and best textual witnesses to the New Testament do not contain the section dealing with the adulterous woman, and no church father before the twelfth century refers to it. To complicate matters further, a number of manuscripts place the story in different locations: some have it after John 7:36, some after John 7:44, some after John 21:25, and some after Luke 21:38. It is clear that the tradition is late and was not fixed in the Gospel of John at its early stage; indeed, it may well have been an independent tradition that was initially added at various points in the already-written Gospels.

But while the story is clearly not part of the "original" Fourth Gospel, it has nonetheless become an important part of the Gospel tradition. Even critical editions leave it in the text, although often annotated, because the story is so well known and in many ways fits what we know of Jesus as portrayed in the rest of the Fourth Gospel.

The story is about a woman accused of adultery by a group of Pharisees and scribes. The narrative says she was caught in the act of adultery and thus liable to the punishment of stoning. The reader is immediately struck by the injustice of the whole arrangement, for it is apparent that if the woman was caught in the act of adultery, then so must the man have been. But only the woman is charged. Moreover, rather than simply seeking justice, the scribes and Pharisees are using this person to entrap Jesus; the accused is a pawn in a dispute between Jesus and the Jewish representatives, not a person due an impartial judgment. In response to this, Jesus suggests simply that the one with no sin should begin the process of giving judgment. When all the accusers have departed, Jesus himself offers no accusation, only the command to go and sin no more. The story speaks to Jesus' message of mercy, the extensive presence of guilt even among the "righteous," and the escalating efforts to entrap Jesus.

One might wonder why this story ended up here, at the end of John 7 and the beginning of John 8. It seems likely that it fits here because of both the rising tide of Jewish opposition to Jesus and the teaching about judgment that follows in chapter 8. There Jesus says that he judges no one, although he clearly has the power and the authority to do so. Chapters 6 and 7 of John also deal more with the Pharisees than most other parts of John. But whatever the reason, the tradition of the adulterous woman was attached to the Fourth Gospel's account of Jesus and has rested securely within its covers for many years.

 Want to Know More?

About messianic expectations? See Celia Brewer Marshall, *A Guide through the New Testament* (Louisville, Ky.: Westminster John Knox Press, 1994), 33.

About the miracles of Jesus? See Arnold B. Rhodes, *The Mighty Acts of God* W. Eugene March (Louisville, Ky.: Geneva Press, 2000), 274–79.

? Questions for Reflection

1. Compare this version of the feeding of the five thousand with Mark 6:30–44; Matthew 14:13–21; and Luke 9:10–17. The similarities are striking. What are the differences?
2. Jesus tells the crowd that they should work for the food that leads to eternal life. Compare this to Jesus' words to the woman at the well. In both cases, it was difficult for the people to understand Jesus' meaning. How would you interpret his meaning to them?
3. Reread John 6:35–40. What does the phrase "I am the bread of life" mean to you? What images does it convey? How has your faith been nourished by this bread?
4. Jesus' words in 8:7 are commonly used today. Have you used this phrase recently? Has anyone said these words to you? What was the situation?

5 John 8:31–9:41

Growing Opposition to Jesus

It is clear that chapter 7 and the beginning of chapter 8 center on the Tabernacles feast, as Jesus utilizes imagery of Tabernacles in self-referential metaphors ("living water," "light of the world") to reveal his true nature to the Jewish festivalgoers. When, though, does the narrative move beyond the Tabernacles feast? The continuation of the discussion with "the Jews" in 8:31–59 is not clearly marked off from the preceding dialogues by any geographical or chronological markers. So are readers to assume that Jesus is still in Jerusalem during or immediately after the Tabernacles festival? Although chapter 8 ends with an attempt on Jesus' life, it is not clear that chapter 9, with the account of the man born blind, is meant to be in the same time period: reference is made to the pool of Siloam, and Jesus reiterates that he is the light of the world. Indeed, the beginning of chapter 10, with the "good shepherd" discourse, has no definite break from what precedes it. We might well consider the Tabernacles controversies to continue all the way to 10:22, when a new festival is introduced—the Dedication festival (or Hanukkah).

> "Just as the whole chapter argues who Jesus is as related to God in the terms proper to the Evangelist's lifetime, so it concludes with the conviction of John's opponents that Jesus' followers are putting him in God's place."—Sloyan, *John*, Interpretation, 111.

Jesus and Abraham (8:31–59)

The initial series of exchanges and discourses at the Tabernacles festival, discussed in the previous unit, resulted in many of the Jews believing in Jesus. But to what degree did they really believe? Was this a passing agreement with Jesus' words, a mere mental assent, or was it a full understanding that Jesus is the one sent from God? It would appear that in the dialogues at the close of chapter 8, Jesus is asking just this question. It is a question that might be posed equally well to all who claim to believe in Jesus: Does one have a lasting faith with substantive implications or simply a passing mental agreement?

Jesus makes the claim that discipleship, true faith, is based on continuing in Jesus' teaching. And this act of remaining in Jesus will result in knowledge of truth and thus freedom from the captivity of sin. The theme of remaining in Jesus, of "abiding" in his words and thoughts, is important in John (cf. John 15:4–16) and reappears in the epistle 1 John as well. Abiding in a teacher's instruction seems natural if a student believes he or she is teaching correctly—that is, if one believes in the teacher. And such an exhortation seems even more reasonable in the case of Jesus, who claimed to be not only a teacher but the one sent from heaven, the one who speaks authoritatively on behalf of the Father.

But in this setting, the audience immediately misinterprets Jesus' statement and fastens on the promise "to be free" as a negative judgment. They invoke the memory and promise of Abraham to claim that they are already free and have always been free—a statement that blithely overlooks the Jewish history in Egypt and in Babylon and even the present occupation of Palestine by the Romans. By denying their enslavement to oppressive forces, whether political or spiritual, the Jews are really disavowing their need to find freedom in Jesus, which negates any affirmation of faith they may have made.

But the conflict over freedom is grounded in something far greater than a failure by the Jewish audience to perceive their past and present enslavement. For Jesus, enslavement is a fundamental spiritual quality, a turning away from God and an obedience to the created order rather than to the heavenly order. It is, in a word, sin. And sin itself is slavery: "Everyone who commits sin is a slave to sin" (8:34). Thus the Jews' response that they are free is itself a denial of the force of sin and evil and thus a failure to acknowledge its power. But in denying its power, people not only fail to acknowledge God but actually serve the darkness, the forces that oppose God. "You are from your father the devil, and you choose to do your father's desires" (8:44). Jesus' argument, then, attempts both to illuminate the spiritual blindness of the Jews and to encourage them to keep his word. The two are, indeed, two sides of the same coin.

The Jews' insistence on their freedom and their invocation of Abraham lead Jesus to question their motives toward him. Certainly, he now engages not only these "believing" Jews but the entire Jewish leadership by criticizing their attempt to kill him. The attempt to kill Jesus makes plain the Jewish leadership's unwillingness to hear God's word from Jesus. And in their protest against remaining in Jesus' word, the audience who would claim to believe has actually aligned itself with Jesus' opponents, not as his disciples. So, for John, the "believing" Jews are really just a part of the broader opposition to Jesus—"the Jews."

> "[The Gospel writer] does not disbelieve in Torah, written or oral, nor does he think it unimportant in illuminating the human scene. He thinks it has been succeeded, however, by the revealer of God who possesses and is himself the Light of life (see v. 5; 8:12). Jesus is the Light that judges and saves the world. He is also a blinding light—not to those who admit their blindness, for to those he gives sight—but to these who proclaim that they see and in their boast of vision are blind."—Sloyan, *John*, Interpretation, 122.

The argument over their relationship to Abraham becomes a metaphor for this much deeper spiritual situation. On the one hand, "the Jews" claim Abraham as their father in response to Jesus' exhortation "Do what you have heard from the Father" (8:38). Their claim that Abraham is their father is an implicit rejection of God as their father. But Jesus presses the point still further: if "the Jews" were indeed Abraham's descendants, then they would act like it, instead of trying to kill Jesus. In this attempt on his life, they actually demonstrate that they are spiritually children of the devil rather than of Abraham (8:44; cf. 8:41). John's strong dualism becomes apparent here: if one does not perceive the truth that comes from God, then that person is not really from God. Rather than being part of the light, that person is exposed as part of the darkness, of which God has no part.

This language is deliberately provocative, and there is a strong reaction. The Jews respond by claiming that Jesus is a Samaritan and has a demon. The Samaritan charge seeks to disconnect Jesus from the "true" descendants of Abraham, and the demon charge connects Jesus with the devil instead of God. The lines have been drawn. While originally counted as "believing," the audience is now clearly part of the disbelieving group called "the Jews." In a final appeal to them to remain in his teaching, Jesus says that by keeping his word the believer will escape death. But this promise, too, is misunderstood, as so many of his statements are misunderstood. For the Jews here, since Abraham, who kept God's word, died, Jesus' statement clearly separates him from them and from the Abrahamic tradition and invalidates his testimony. There seems to be no way for Jesus' arguments to reach them; each statement is misunderstood and results in further disbelief.

In the culmination of the argument, Jesus defends his teaching by fully identifying himself with Abraham. Abraham, Jesus says, rejoiced to see the day of Jesus' appearance. In other words, Abraham is alive (with God?), not dead, and he thus experiences the present situation. But Jesus' statement only deepens the misunderstanding, for the Jews have already said Abraham died; how can he possibly rejoice over Jesus? But Jesus adds one final comment, which makes sense only if he was the preexistent Word of God: "Before Abraham was, I am." By saying "I am" about a time long before his birth, he appears to be claiming the title YHWH (Yahweh)—for the Hebrew name for God is based on the verb *to be,* perhaps meaning "I am who I am" (cf. Exod. 3:13–15).

Healing the blind man

And so, as each controversial teaching seems to escalate the conflict between Jesus and "the Jews," they take up stones to try and kill him. What began as professed belief in Jesus actually develops into a murder attempt. It is apparent they are not willing to continue in Jesus' word but rather depart from it immediately when they do not hear what they want to hear.

The Man Born Blind (9:1–41)

In the aftermath of the Tabernacles controversies (7:10–8:30), after his argument of who can best claim a relationship with Abraham, Jesus performs another miraculous action that produces a controversy between him and "the Jews." Like Jesus' healing of the paralytic (5:2–18), the healing of the blind man is performed on the Sabbath and results in a strenuous disagreement over the propriety of healing on the Sabbath. Within the Gospel, this story contains a number of themes that are central to John's portrayal of Jesus and that also point to the growing hostility between Jesus and the Jewish leadership. At the same time, from a historical perspective, the story of the healing of the blind man raises serious questions about the setting of the Gospel's writing and about the audience to whom it was written.

A. The Healing Itself

Jesus heals the blind man as he is walking through Jerusalem. It is possible that the setting is still close to the time of the Tabernacles; there has been no narrative reference to a long passage of time. Jesus is still in the Jerusalem area, since the blind man is instructed to wash his eyes in the pool of Siloam. It is interesting that Siloam is the pool from which the water libations were taken during Tabernacles. And it is interesting that Jesus draws again on the "light" metaphor in this healing ("I am the light of the world"), which is reminiscent of his declaration in the Tabernacles feast (cf. 8:12, "I am the light of the world"). It is likely, with these elements present, that we are dealing with traditions closely tied to Jesus' actions during the Tabernacles feast.

Whatever the timing of the event, Jesus is prompted by his disciples to discuss the origin of the blind man's disability. Whose sin is it? No one actually asks Jesus to heal the man: not the disciples, not the blind man, not others in the crowd. Jesus responds to the initial question by spitting on the ground and smearing a paste on the eyes of the man and telling him to wash in the pool of Siloam. Upon doing so, the blind man gains his sight.

The miracle story is reminiscent of the importance healing the blind plays in the other Gospels:

1. A blind man is healed at Bethsaida using spittle in the eye (Mark 8:22–26).
2. A blind man on the road to Jericho (Bartimaeus in Mark) is healed when Jesus has pity on him (Matt. 20:29–34; Mark 10:46–52; Luke 18:35–43).
3. Two blind men are healed (Matt. 9:27–31).
4. A blind and mute man with a demon is healed of both disabilities and the demon is cast out (Matt. 12:22–30).
5. Jesus' quotation of Isaiah 61:1–2 in his programmatic sermon at Nazareth (Luke 4:18) suggests that curing blindness is a sign of the messianic age.

6. Certain summary statements suggest this is an important part of Jesus' ministry: Luke's summary of Jesus' ministry delivered to John the Baptist (Luke 7:21–22) and Matthew's report of healings in the Temple (Matt. 21:14).

But while healing the blind is a central feature of Jesus' healing ministry in all the Gospels, John's presentation here is significantly different. First of all, nobody asks for the healing. No one calls out for healing or mercy. Jesus heals the man in response to a theological question, not a plea for mercy. Second, Jesus uses a paste of mud to effect the healing. This is similar to Mark's description of Jesus using his spittle to heal a blind man, but here Jesus mixes his spittle with dirt to produce the healing agent. Moreover, in John's Gospel the man goes to the pool of Siloam to wash as the final stage of the miracle. Third, only in John is the man born blind. For the Fourth Gospel, this feature is important, for it is used to underscore the magnitude of the miracle. Finally, the reaction to the miracle, at least at the beginning, is remarkably low key. The man is healed, but he does not rush back to find Jesus and seems at a loss to know how his healing came about. His answers to the initial questioning about the healing are subdued and understated. In answer to who he thinks it was who healed him, the blind man simply responds, "A prophet." The net effect of this curious healing is to suggest that there is more to the story—which there is, as the narrative continues to unfold.

> ### From Blindness to Sight
>
> "Amazing grace, how sweet the sound, that saved a wretch like me! I once was lost, but now am found, was blind, but now I see."—John Newton, "Amazing Grace, How Sweet the Sound."
>
> "One thing I do know, that though I was blind, now I see" (John 9:25).
>
> "Jesus said, 'I came into this world for judgment so that those who do not see may see, and those who do see may become blind'" (John 9:39).

B. The Relationship between Sin and Disability

The theological discussion that initiated the healing concerned the relationship of sin to physical disability and suffering. A man born blind was used as an example for Jesus. The question "Who sinned, he or his parents?" presumes that physical disability is the result of sin. This connection has antecedents in the wisdom tradition, where prosperity and health are indications of righteousness and illness and poverty are indications of sin. The perceived relationship between sin and suffering can be seen in Job's three friends' accusations that Job's difficulties must come from some hidden sin (cf. Job 8, 15, 18). In this case, the question is not "Did he sin?" but, since the blindness was from birth, "Who sinned?"

Jesus, however, does not accept the premise on which the question is based. It is not an issue of sin but rather of whether illness can be used as an occasion to do God's work. Jesus turns the discussion from a theological to an ethical one: Are we doing the works of God?

In his response to the disciples and in his instruction to the blind man, Jesus once again links his discussion to the Tabernacles feast, particularly to his discourses that dominated the previous several chapters of John. Recall that on the final day of the feast, Jesus used two elements of the Tabernacles rituals to disclose himself to the people: using the ritual of the water drawn from Siloam and poured out on the altar, Jesus said he would provide living water that would flow out of the believer; and comparing himself to the candle lights arraying the temple area, Jesus said he was truly the light of the world. Echoes of these return in this healing. On hearing the question about the blind man, Jesus once again says that he is the light of the world. And he then sends the blind man to wash in the pool of Siloam, the same pool from which the water libation was drawn. Perhaps these references are an indication that this miracle is set on the final day of the Tabernacles feast. Or perhaps the themes that were introduced there are so compelling they continue to overshadow the narrative as it develops.

C. The Examination of the Healed Man

But the healing of the blind man is only the first act in this complex story. Initially, the neighbors of the blind man are perplexed when they see him sighted. Hardly able to believe it, they keep asking one another if this can be the man who was blind, while he keeps asserting that it really is he. In response to the question of how he came to see, the man can only recite the basic story told in the healing account. All he knows is that Jesus healed him; he did what Jesus said.

When the neighbors bring the blind man to the Pharisees, the same basic question is asked, and the blind man again tells the story. But two crucial complexities are added in the second telling that determine the direction of the narrative. First, the narrator tells us for the first time that this occurred on the Sabbath. With the background of the controversy surrounding the healing at the Sheep Pool, Bethesda, in chapter 5, the reader is instantly aware of the problem. Second, the blind man tells in more detail how he was healed: Jesus put mud in his eyes, then when he washed it he could see. In early Judaism, the making of mud was a violation of the Sabbath—understood as a rather specific violation. Thus the Pharisees seize on this violation as an indication that Jesus cannot be from God. But the perplexing issue is raised: How could Jesus perform such a healing if he is a sinner? There is, then, a split in opinion among the Pharisees. And the blind man simply understands Jesus to be a prophet— the first term that seems to arise in John when people are confronted with his actions.

"The Jews," who may include some of the Pharisees, seem to be in this instance simply the opponents of Jesus, as they are unwilling to let the matter lie. They next seek to show that the blind man was not really blind from birth. But the parents confirm that he was born blind. However, on being asked questions about the healing, they refuse to answer, for "they were afraid of the Jews; for the Jews had already agreed that anyone who confessed Jesus to be the Messiah would be put out of the synagogue" (9:22). This particular statement has raised some interesting historical questions relative to the composition of the Gospel, which we will consider later. But within the development of the story, this statement returns the readers to the pattern of behavior on the part of "the Jews." They have been trying to arrest or kill Jesus in the preceding narratives (5:18; 7:1, 32; 8:59), and now we learn that they have also been persecuting those who confessed Jesus as Messiah. What might have been simply a disagreement about healing takes on the aura of persecution and danger that increasingly is the pervasive feature in "the Jews'" attitude toward Jesus and his followers.

> "The Pharisees have enough spiritual knowledge and insight to be held responsible for rejecting Jesus. Their sin remains, for they did not act on their best insights but acted like the blind. Like a person who witnesses a crime being committed and knows the right thing to do is report it but turns a blind eye, they have chosen darkness rather than light."—Witherington, *John's Wisdom*, 185.

Getting no adequate answer from the parents, "the Jews" return to examining the blind man. Their desire is to get the man who had been blind to acknowledge Jesus to be a sinner. But the man born blind is unwilling to consider this seriously. He simply knows that he was blind and that now he can see, and in his mind it is difficult to imagine a sinner having such power. He turns to slight mocking of "the Jews," first by asking them if they wish to be disciples (9:27) and then by challenging their claim not to know where Jesus comes from

(9:30–33). For him, this question is simple—only someone who comes "from God" could heal a man born blind.

The controversy with "the Jews" ends where the healing story began. They dismiss the man as a man "born entirely in sins," which tells the reader that they consider him a sinner because of his former blindness. Apparently, even the fact that he has been healed will not change their opinion of him.

D. The Response of Faith

John continues the story, however, beyond the failed examination by the Pharisees and "the Jews." Once all the attackers have left, the stage lights are turned on Jesus and the man who was blind, with a group of Pharisees gathered around the periphery. Now that the furor has died down, Jesus can call for a response of faith: "Do you believe in the Son of Man?" (9:36). Once Jesus identifies himself as this Son of Man, the man who was once blind responds immediately with a confession ("Lord, I believe") and with worship. It is implied that the blind man, as a result, is free of sin. But by the same word of judgment, the Pharisees are characterized as being blind and full of sin: "If you were blind, you would not have sin. But now that you say, 'We see,' your sin remains."

Here the crisis of faith is displayed in its full and complete form. On the one hand, the crisis (meaning a situation that demands a defining decision) that arises out of the miraculous healing finds the blind man openly confessing Jesus and worshiping him. His decision and response are appropriate and validated (he is healthy and free of sin). On the other hand, "the Jews" and the Pharisees, who are increasingly seen as almost the same group, fail to respond to the situation with faith. They are now seen as spiritually blind and full of sin. And correspondingly, the blind man's parents are seen as afraid and discouraged; they do not oppose Jesus, but they fail to respond to the crisis of decision.

E. The Historical Setting of the Story

John 9 has become a crucial chapter for interpreting the Fourth Gospel because of the difficulty of the image of "the Jews" casting people out of the synagogue during Jesus' lifetime. In light of this difficulty, J. Louis Martyn suggests that this passage says more about the time the Gospel was written than about Jesus' own lifetime. He suggests the passage should be read on two levels: the level of the narra-

tive itself, in which Jesus and the blind man are opposed and perse-
cuted, and the level of the evangelist's situation. It is in the latter situation that Martyn would place the circumstance of casting out of
the synagogue. He suggests that this began to occur in about 85 C.E.
with the introduction of a curse in the Eighteen Benedictions read in
the synagogue: "Cursed are the heretics and the Nazareans." This
curse, the *birkhat ha-minim*, would have identified anyone who stood
up in the synagogue to read the benedictions as a Christian, for a
Christian would have been unable to voice such a curse and so would
become apparent to the congregation. This, then, would have
resulted in that individual being removed from the synagogue.

As attractive as this theory seems—and it has the general assent of
many, if not most, Johannine scholars—there are real problems that
should be addressed:

1. There is very little evidence that the *birkhat ha-minim* was introduced in the period Martyn suggests, that the Jewish council at
   Jamnia could have ordered it read in synagogues of the time,
   that it was widely used in synagogues, or that it even refers to
   Christians (the few texts we have are not clear).
2. There is certainly evidence of scattered reaction against Christians
   in certain Jewish communities, as both the book of Acts and
   Justin Martyr would suggest. This may have happened early, not
   later, as a result of occasional reaction against the Jesus movement.
3. If the Gospel were written with this "two-level" approach, one
   might expect the presentation of other occasions in which those
   who are believers in Jesus are in danger of being cast out of the synagogues. But in the raising of Lazarus, for instance, Mary and
   Martha are accompanied by many of "the Jews," and no retribution is
   ever directed at them. So the Gospel itself does not demonstrate
   a thoroughgoing concern for such a dual reading.

 Want to Know More?

About healing on the Sabbath? See Michael R. Cosby, *Portraits of Jesus* (Louisville, Ky.: Westminster John Knox Press, 1999), 93.

About the biblical image of seeing? See Leland Ryken, James C. Wilhoit, and Tremper Longman III, eds., *Dictionary of Biblical Imagery* (Downers Grove, Ill.: InterVarsity Press, 1998), 255–56.

So, while the threat of being cast out of the synagogue in John 9:22
seems a bit unusual and may be somewhat anachronistic, it is not
apparent that this verse unlocks the key to John's origin or to its

meaning. It is preferable instead to see the incident as just one feature in the developing conflict between "the Jews" and Jesus. It would be worthwhile, then, to examine a bit more closely the pattern of this developing conflict in the Fourth Gospel.

The Growing Conflict between "the Jews" and Jesus

The healing of the blind man in chapter 9 brings to a head a pattern of increasing conflict between Jesus and the group called by John simply "the Jews." We can briefly trace the outlines of this pattern:

- In chapter 2, at the Temple incident, the first indication of opposition is seen by the emergence of a group called "the Jews" with their questioning of Jesus' action in the Temple and their consternation at his prediction of the Temple's destruction (2:18–20).
- Following the exchange with Nicodemus in chapter 3, "the Jews" seek to clarify Jesus' relationship with John the Baptist (3:25–26).
- At the unnamed feast of the Jews in chapter 5, "the Jews" take issue with Jesus' healing of the paralytic at the pool near the Sheep Gate. The controversy here deals with Sabbath healing. John notes that this created an ongoing opposition, even to the point of desiring Jesus' death (5:18).
- In the discourses that follow the feeding of the five thousand, "the Jews" murmur because Jesus says he is the bread come down from heaven (6:41).
- The introduction to the Tabernacles narrative (7:1) reminds the reader that "the Jews" sought to kill Jesus. Their sphere of influence is apparently in the southern region, Judea.
- At the Feast of Tabernacles, "the Jews" are looking for Jesus, and the people are wary of speaking about him "for fear of the Jews" (7:11–13).
- The Pharisees and chief priests send officials to arrest Jesus, but they fail to do so (7:32, 45–46).
- In the controversy over Abraham in chapter 8, "the Jews" conclude the exchange by taking up stones to throw at Jesus, but he escapes (8:59).
- The story of the healing of the blind man in chapter 9 informs the reader that "the Jews" had agreed to exclude from the synagogue anyone who confessed Jesus as the Christ.

It is clear that the Fourth Evangelist tells a story of increasing opposition, mainly from the group called "the Jews." This group is apparently more powerful in Judea than elsewhere and is often closely related to the Pharisees and chief priests, although these latter groups are distinguished at times. (See the discussion of the composition of "the Jews" in Unit 2.)

But even if we can't determine exactly who "the Jews" are—and it appears that John has intended the term to be a bit vague—it is clear that John presents a narrative of increasing opposition to Jesus. With the healing of the blind man, the stage is set. Jesus has come to declare himself to the people of Israel. But with each revelation of his nature, "the Jews" react with opposition, even violence. The narrative hints even now at one aspect of the conclusion to the story—the tragic death of Jesus because of the opposition of those who refuse to know him. And yet John also portrays the ultimate revelation of Jesus' nature in the very midst of opposition. His "glorification" will be complete on the cross—the ultimate sign of his divine nature and mission. So opposition is never victorious but allows Jesus to reveal himself more completely to those who are open to God's activity in the midst of humanity.

 ## Questions for Reflection

1. The author says that the question Jesus is asking in 8:31–59 should be asked to all who claim to believe in Jesus: Does one have a lasting faith—a full understanding of Jesus as the one sent from God—or merely a passing agreement with Jesus' words? How would you attempt to answer that question?
2. Jesus claims, "Before Abraham was, I am" (8:58), further escalating the conflict with the Jews. Discuss what Jesus meant by this.
3. Read some of the other Gospel stories of blindness. (See the list on pages 56–57.) What is the significance of blindness to Jesus' ministry? Is there blindness among Jesus' followers still? How so?
4. This unit treats the tension between Jesus and the religious establishment of his day. What would the tensions be today if Jesus were to come to church?

John 10–11

I Am the Good Shepherd;
I Am the Resurrection and the Life

The structure of chapter 10 presents some initial problems for the reader with respect to how one should read its various units in the context of the·continuing narrative of the Fourth Gospel. The parable of the good shepherd, introduced with Jesus' "Amen, amen" statement in 10:1, follows immediately on the disagreement with the Pharisees in 9:39–41. Without any indication of a passage of time or a change of location, the "good shepherd" discourse of 10:1–21 would appear to be intended as a continuation of the disputes that followed the blind man's healing. That this is the nature of the story seems to find confirmation in the conclusion of the shepherd discourse: there is again a division among "the Jews," in which various themes from chapters 8 and 9 are raised again.

In particular, in 10:19–21, we hear once again, on the one hand, that Jesus must have a demon and, on the other hand, that this is hardly possible given that he was able to heal a blind man. The reader of the Gospel will recall that similar statements were made in the preceding Tabernacles controversies: Jesus was accused of having a demon in 8:48–52, and his ability to heal a blind man was raised as a defense against his being a sinner at 9:16 and 9:32–33. As a result of this concluding statement, the whole shepherd discourse in 10:1–18 becomes literarily connected to the dialogue between Jesus and "the Jews" in chapter 9.

Despite this indication of narrative unity, it has been proposed that there was some dislocation in the text. In the subsequent scene, which begins with the festival of Dedication (10:22), Jesus again returns to the theme of being the shepherd. Based on this, it has been proposed that verses 19–21 have been displaced and probably should be the conclusion of chapter 9, and that originally the units of text dealing with the shepherd theme (10:1–18 and 10:22–30) were connected, perhaps in a geographical and chronological context distinct from chapter 9. In other words, the existence of the shepherd theme is said to have been all of one piece, falling logically after the conclusion of the Tabernacles context and probably in the context of the Feast of Dedication.

Although the shepherd image is used in two separate settings in John 10, it is unnecessary to propose dislocation of text. The narrative as presented in John is coherent. We have seen in the preceding dialogues at the Tabernacles feast that Jesus uses a variety of metaphors to illustrate who he is, and at times he returns to a previous image. So the metaphor of "light to the world" occurs in 8:12 and then is reintroduced in a new setting, that of the healing of the blind man in 9:5. So also, the recurrence of the shepherd imagery in a subsequent setting is not surprising and need not indicate textual displacement.

But John's use of the "shepherd" metaphor in a variety of settings does suggest that it is important for our understanding of Jesus' message and mission. Indeed, the metaphor draws on a rich tradition in Old Testament texts and serves both to interpret and further to develop the conflict between Jesus and "the Jews," as well as to suggest the close relationship Jesus seeks with those who would believe.

> "For thus says the Lord GOD: I myself will search for my sheep, and will seek them out. As shepherds seek out their flocks when they are among their scattered sheep, so I will seek out my sheep. I will rescue them from all the places to which they have been scattered on a day of clouds and thick darkness. I will bring them out from the peoples and gather them from the countries, and will bring them into their own land; and I will feed them on the mountains of Israel, by the watercourses, and in all the inhabited parts of the land. . . . I myself will be the shepherd of my sheep, and I will make them lie down, says the Lord GOD"—(Ezek. 34:11–13, 15).

The True Shepherd and the Thief (10:1–6)

The parable of the shepherd begins with a description of sheep in a sheepfold. Two main characters are contrasted: thieves and the true shepherd. On the one hand, thieves who would harm the sheep try to gain entrance by means other than the gate, for the gatekeeper would recognize them as illegitimate and bar entry. In contrast, the true shepherd of the sheep enters by the gate. The gatekeeper recognizes him as the proper shepherd and gives him entrance. Furthermore, the sheep recognize him and follow him.

The parable uses shepherd imagery to contrast two different groups who would attempt to lead the sheep. It is clear, as Jesus further develops the story, that the images of shepherd/thief and the flock are being used to contrast true leaders with false leaders and to apply this image to their relationship with the people of Israel. This imagery is not original with Jesus; he is drawing on concepts found in the Old Testament scriptures.

In numerous places God is described as a shepherd and the people of Israel as a flock: Psalms 23 and 80; Isaiah 40:11; Jeremiah 39:10; and, in the images' most extensive form, Ezekiel 34:11–16. But the sheep/shepherd imagery is also used in the Old Testament to describe false shepherds, or those who would deplete the flock and lead them astray: Jeremiah 10:21; 12:10; 23:1–2; Zechariah 10:3; 11:15; Zephaniah 3:3; and again in Ezekiel 34, where the good shepherd is contrasted with the evil shepherd.

The imagery of the shepherd is used a third way in the Old Testament, to describe a future leader who will serve as a good shepherd; this echoes how God is described in the first group of scriptures cited above. In the third group we find Psalm 78:70–72; Micah 5:4; Zechariah 13:7–9; Jeremiah 3:15; 23:4–6; and Ezekiel 34.

It is not unlikely, then, that these images drawn from the Old Testament, especially from Ezekiel 34, provide the interpretive framework that is assumed for this parable in John. Jesus draws on this imagery and expects his audience to hear the references to Ezekiel as a backdrop to his own statements. There is even a striking similarity in the order of the images presented by Ezekiel and Jesus. For instance, Ezekiel 34 begins with a judgment on false rulers who have not cared for the flock but instead have scattered them and allowed them to fall prey to wild animals. In a

"I will set up over them one shepherd, my servant David, and he shall feed them: he shall feed them and be their shepherd. And I, the LORD, will be their God, and my servant David shall be prince among them; I, the LORD have spoken" (Ezek. 34:23–24; cf. 37:24).

similar way, the Fourth Evangelist has Jesus begin his parable with a focus on those who would attempt to gain access to the sheep for their own gain—the thief and bandit. Ezekiel 34 then turns to the proper shepherd, God, who truly cares for the sheep. In the same way, the parable in John 10 follows up the discussion of the thieves with a discussion of the true shepherd, who is known by the gatekeeper and by the sheep and shepherds them with concern and individual care.

In many ways, then, the parable in John 10:1–5 is a shortened summary of Ezekiel 34. But even with this interpretive backdrop, the parable is not simply duplicating Ezekiel's imagery or that of other Old Testament passages but is drawing on them to develop a new, rich metaphor. At the same time, however, Jesus' parable often presents some confusing imagery, almost as if there is a surplus of meaning in the parable. Who is the gatekeeper? And what is the relationship of gatekeeper to shepherd? In the shepherd discourse, Jesus does not draw the analogy too tightly; the central feature is paramount, and any attempt to overinterpret the metaphor distracts from its clear warning against false leaders.

Jesus as the Gate (10:7–10)

The parable in its sparse form is difficult to interpret, even against the backdrop of Ezekiel 34. It would appear that, given the sharp exchange with the Pharisees in 9:39–41, the reader should understand the Pharisees to be implicated as the "thieves and bandits," but this is not absolutely clear. And so the narrative informs the reader that he or she is not really expected to understand all the implications—after all, the figure of speech was not understandable to its first audience either (10:6)! The parable must be further interpreted to make sense of it. And yet the basic parable is crucial for the whole section, for it provides a foundation on which the subsequent interpretations are based.

What follows, then, in verses 7–18, is Jesus' interpretation of the parable, in which various elements in the parable are applied to Jesus himself. Indeed, it is striking that in the interpretation, Jesus does not begin with a consideration of the "thieves and bandits"; rather, he identifies himself as the gate of the sheepfold. This is somewhat curious, since the gate has hardly been the focus of the preceding parable. But by identifying himself as the gate, he proclaims himself to be the sole legitimate means of access to the sheep. This serves to provide a sharp contrast to the means of access the "thieves and bandits" must use to get into the sheepfold.

> "The view Jesus has of these 'other sheep' is therefore not only benign but hopeful. They do not know him but they will."—Sloyan, *John*, Interpretation, 132.

When he turns, then, to consider the "thieves and bandits," they are contrasted with Jesus in two ways: (1) he represents the legitimate leadership, while thieves and bandits are clearly illegitimate and contrary to what is proper; and (2) he comes to save and protect, but thieves and bandits come only to kill and destroy. On the latter theme, Jesus returns to one of his previous topics, that he is a life giver. We have seen this in many forms already: in the Prologue (1:40), where the Word is life; in Jesus' discussion with Nicodemus (3:15); in his exchange with the woman of Samaria (4:14); in the discourse following the healing of the paralytic (5:24); and after the feeding of the five thousand (6:47). Jesus gives life, true life, and this must be contrasted to the result of false leadership. Jesus leads people to a true understanding of God, while false leaders draw away from apprehending the reality of God.

Jesus as the Good Shepherd (10:11–21)

With verses 11–21, Jesus brings the implications of the previous parable to their logical conclusion, although a conclusion that must have been unsettling to the leaders of the Jewish people. This conclusion emphasizes four elements: (1) Jesus' own future role as one who will give up his life on behalf of humanity; (2) the current leaders' interests, which are said to be primarily focused on personal gain rather than concern for the people; (3) Jesus' claim of intimate knowledge of "his own," in the same way that he and God share intimate knowledge of each other; and (4) a recognition that others outside Israel are to be brought into the flock.

That Jesus will die has been broached only once previously in the Fourth Gospel—at the conclusion of the Temple incident (2:22), when the narrator tells us that the disciples remembered his words after he was raised from the dead. Now, in this section, Jesus introduces a major theme of his dying on behalf of his people. This statement serves a purpose in John's Gospel similar to the purpose Jesus' predictions of his passion serve in the Synoptic Gospels (e.g., Mark 8:31; 9:31; 10:32): to begin to orient the reader to the central role the death and resurrection play. It is important that John portrays Jesus predicting not only his death but also his resurrection (10:17). This, then, foreshadows the passion narrative to

> "Jesus, in obedient dependence on the Father, can give life to whom he will. The life is that which the Gospel features throughout. It is not simply a physical being alive but having as a gift from Jesus the life which he has from his Father."—Sloyan, *John*, Interpretation, 144.

come. In this acknowledgment of his coming death, the real danger of the increasing opposition of "the Jews," whom we have seen are escalating their attempts to arrest or even to kill him, is underscored. We know from Jesus' own words that these are not false threats but are a real tension in the story—Jesus' *giving* of life to the world is somehow closely related to his *giving up* his own life. But that death is not the end of the story; it is a beginning.

At the same time, however, this section continues the strong dualism between the "good shepherd" and those who are, by implication, "bad shepherds." Previously this contrast was illustrated as between one who enters through the gate (v. 2) and the thief or robber, who enters by another way (v. 1) and who comes to kill and destroy (v. 10). In verses 11–18, Jesus shifts the image to the shepherd who willingly guards the sheep, as contrasted with one who works simply for money. The contrast raises the question of which shepherd actually cares for the well-being of the sheep. The shifting metaphor serves to highlight the polemical nature of the discourse: Jesus is criticizing the leadership of Israel. While "the Jews" have been attacking Jesus, he also is engaging in a verbal attack on their leadership. In this polemic, Jesus clearly echoes Ezekiel's prophecy against the leaders of Israel.

The contrast between Jesus and the "bad" shepherds of Israel has further implications. One facet of Jesus' shepherd role is his close identification with the sheep, the people of Israel. This is illustrated through the aspect of "knowing." Jesus "knows" his sheep, and they in turn "know" him. This implies that those who don't "know" him, that is, who don't believe in him, are not his own. Their very refusal to acknowledge Jesus as Christ has defined their status with respect to him. But believers' "knowing" Jesus is not in fact the first movement; rather, Jesus "knows" his own first, and his own simply respond in

> ### Key Terms
>
> *Pharisees:* The Gospel portrait is slanted against this group, mostly presenting them as hypocrites and opponents of Jesus. A more accurate portrait shows them to be a priestly group whose heritage might trace back to the lawyers. Often sectarian in their practices, particularly with respect to diet, ritual purity, and Sabbath observance, the Pharisees were well respected as leaders.
>
> *Sanhedrin:* The ruling body of Jews, composed of chief priests, scribes, and elders, primarily responsible for making judgments and collecting the Temple tax.

kind. Knowing, of course, has a sense of mental grasp of facts, but is deeper than that—here it suggests a deep acceptance and comfort. Like the word *abide,* the word *know* implies a deep sense of belonging and identification with the object. We have seen this in the Prologue, where two parallel statements say much the same thing:

1:10 He was in the world, and the world came into being through him; yet the world did not know him.

1:11 He came to what was his own, and his own people did not accept him.

Jesus knows his sheep, and he belongs to them and remains with them and for them. Similarly, and in response, his sheep know him, and they identify with him and belong to him.

This play on the verb *to know* is heightened by the way in which Jesus compares his relationship with those who identify with him to his own relationship with God. In just the same way that Jesus "knows" his people and they "know" him, so also God "knows" Jesus and Jesus "knows" God. Notice that, once again, the order of "knowing" is important. First God knows Jesus, and Jesus thus knows God. There is a reciprocity, but the reciprocity has an order, a priority. The priority is placed on God, and Jesus demonstrates the response; in the same way, Jesus first knows his people, and his people respond to him. These examples of mutual "knowing" also suggests a deep intimacy between Jesus and God, an intimacy that is greater than simply "knowing about." The image of the shepherd willing to die for the sheep is deeply intimate, and the same intimacy characterizes God's relationship with Jesus and Jesus' with his people.

Finally, this concluding segment of the shepherd discourse adds a note that could have been deeply troubling to a Jewish audience. Jesus says that other sheep in other folds will become part of his flock. This must surely imply the inclusion of non-Jews into the people of God. In one respect, this idea is not new. Jewish prophecy had long anticipated that all peoples would be united in worshiping God (cf. Jer. 3:15–17; Ezek. 34:23; Mic. 5:3–5; Zech. 14:16–21). But this unity was usually seen in the context of Israel's victorious battle against the nations. Jesus instead is suggesting that some of Israel and some of the nations will become his flock and respond to his voice. There is little of nationalistic triumphalism here, rather a simple acknowledgment that some non-Israelites will also participate in this intimate relationship of "knowing" Jesus and being "known" by him.

Given the sharply dualistic portrayal of the role of shepherd, the particularly intimate portrait of Jesus' relationship with God, and the implication that non-Jews would be part of this special relationship, it is not surprising that conflict was again the result. In 7:12, 25–27, and 31, as well as in 7:40–41, the people are seen as having two minds about Jesus; in 9:16, the Pharisees are divided on how to categorize this Jesus. Here, even "the Jews" are divided in their estimation of Jesus. Some perceive these words as threatening and hence claim that Jesus has a demon. Others are still influenced by the sign of the healing of the blind man and are less willing to claim demonic forces at work in Jesus. But whether ascribing Jesus' words to demonic inspiration or not, the powerful discourse of the good shepherd seems to fall on deaf ears among "the Jews," and the passage only anticipates the subsequent effort to kill him.

At the Feast of the Dedication (10:22–42)

The subsequent scene opens with another Jewish festival, the Feast of the Dedication. This is our modern holiday of Hanukkah, which celebrates the rededication of the Temple after its sacrilege under Antiochus Epiphanes IV in 167 B.C.E.

But while the introductory verse has signaled a change in time, the dialogue in the subsequent narrative still shows strong links to the preceding events. The exchange between the Jews and Jesus in the opening paragraph is based on the previous discourse of the good shepherd. The Jews ask Jesus directly if he is the Christ, and his response returns to the imagery of sheep and "belonging" that marked the shepherd discourse. Using the metaphor of a flock, Jesus declares that he has already told them

> ### What Was the Rededication of the Temple?
>
> In 167 B.C.E., Antiochus Epiphanes IV, the king of the ruling Seleucid dynasty, offered a sacrifice to Zeus within the Temple. After a guerilla war by the sons of Mattathias, especially with the effort of his son Judas (the Maccabee), Jerusalem was freed, and the Temple was rededicated to God in the winter (mid-December) of 164 B.C.E. It is this festival in memory of the rededication of the Temple (the festival that has become the modern-day Hanukkah) that establishes the setting for 10:22–39.

that he is the Christ; the fact that they still ask this only makes it clear that they are not part of his flock. And Jesus, echoing 10:15, returns to the theme of his intimacy with God by stating flatly, "The Father and I are one" (10:30).

With this verse, the thrust of Jesus' unfolding ministry is made clear; yet it only reiterates what the Fourth Evangelist has already illustrated about Jesus. We will recall that, in John 5, Jesus was already accused of equating himself with God. In response to that charge, Jesus sought to show that he did nothing independent of God, and indeed, his authority was derived from God. So without denying his equality with God, in 5:19–30, Jesus seeks to link his work and authority to God as the one who sent him. Here, at the close of the controversies that occur before the final passion, Jesus is once again charged with blasphemy for asserting his close connection with God. Jesus' statement that he and God are one brings about an attempt to stone him. And the rationale for that attempt on his life is based on the implication drawn from Jesus' statement that he and God are one—the implication being that Jesus was making himself God (v. 33).

In defending against the charge of blasphemy, Jesus again does not deny his basic equality with God. Instead, he points to the validity of his work—a proof of his identity and his relationship with God. By doing God's works, he validates his own work. His works, his signs, point to his identity. In them he reveals his glory, his equality with God, his status as Son of God. In John 5, Jesus defended himself by pointing to God's witness in the scriptures; here he defends himself by pointing to God's nature manifested in his good works. By testing the works, Jesus asserts, one can know if Jesus is "of God." "But if I do them [the works of God], even though you do not believe me, believe the works that you may know and understand that the Father is in me and I am in the Father" (10:38).

The conclusion to John 10, then, returns to the point made in John 5. The festival controversies (focused on the unnamed feast of chapter 5, the Tabernacles feast in chapters 7–9, and the Feast of the Dedication in chapter 10) have all dealt with "the Jews'" challenge to Jesus' self-revelation. Jesus has sought by numerous means to demonstrate his relationship with God in a way that is consonant with the Old Testament scriptures, yet recognizing his unique status with God. But at each point Jesus has been met with opposition by "the Jews." The culmination of this opposition is reached in 10:31–39, where "the Jews" seek to stone him and arrest him. The narrative demonstrates a growing momentum to the opposition, a momentum that will reach its apex in the raising of Lazarus and the reaction of "the Jews" to that sign.

Jesus and Lazarus (11:1–44)

The story of Lazarus's raising is well known. Jesus hears about Lazarus's illness and, after a short delay, arrives in Bethany after he has already died. Jesus then raises Lazarus from the dead, even though he has been dead four days. The raising is thus a dramatic demonstration of Jesus' power over life and death. It is, in many ways, the penultimate sign of his connection with God, for in reviving someone who has been dead this long, Jesus manifests an almost creative power over the world. The ultimate sign, of course, is the resurrection, when Jesus shows that he even has the power to take up his own life again.

That the Fourth Evangelist wants to emphasize this raising of Lazarus as a dramatic "sign" is made clear by Jesus' deliberate two-day delay before going to heal Lazarus. The delay is framed so as to give an occasion for a demonstration, or sign, of God's glory in and through the action of Jesus. Jesus says this illness "does not lead to death; rather it is for God's glory, so that the Son of God may be glorified through it" (11:4). As the story progresses, we find that Lazarus actually does die, contrary to this statement of Jesus. But since Lazarus is ultimately raised back to life, Jesus' statement that this sickness "does not lead to death" is still true. The dramatic nature of this raising is indeed a sign of Jesus' life-giving power and his mastery of the creative power of God. It is ultimately a sign pointing to the coming resurrection, made manifest in the present time by Jesus himself. The future is thus given a tangible witness in Jesus' action.

The narrative of Lazarus is built around two ironic wordplays that give it much of its explanatory power. The first wordplay deals with Jesus' use of "sleeping" and "death," which the disciples, reasonably, misinterpret. Their lack of understanding is not a case of lack of faith but simply flows from Jesus' own statements. Jesus has said that the illness would not lead to death (v. 4), so when he says that Lazarus is sleeping (v. 11) and he will go to wake him, the disciples naturally assume that Jesus refers to normal sleep. But sleep can also be a metaphor for death, and so Jesus must clarify that misunderstanding. The wordplay serves to amplify Jesus' delay and to make the raising from the dead all the more dramatic.

The second wordplay deals with the term *rise again,* or *resurrect.* The same word is used to denote different meanings in the dialogue that ensues. When Jesus says, "Your brother will rise again" in verse 23, he uses the same verb *to raise* (*anastesetai*) that Martha uses in her response, "I know that he will rise again in the resurrection on the last day." But again, there is a difference in emphasis. Jesus is speaking of the imminent resurrection of Lazarus in the present day, not the coming eschatological (end-times) resurrection. The confusion over these two different kinds of resurrection, however, implies that Lazarus's resurrection is at least a foreshadowing of the coming general resurrection. And the confusion allows Jesus to assert his authority over both kinds of resurrection: "I am the resurrection and the life" (11:25). Life and death are under the control of Jesus, and the believer participates in the victory over death. Lazarus's resurrection, then, is part of something much greater—the believers' escape from death. But just as Lazarus did die, it is also implied that others will die (even as Jesus himself would die)—but not forever.

Want to Know More?

About biblical imagery of shepherds? See Paul J. Achtemeier, ed., *HarperCollins Bible Dictionary*, rev. ed. (New York: Harper-Collins, 1996), 1012–13.

About Jewish understandings of death and resurrection in the time of Jesus? See Werner H. Schmidt, *The Faith of the Old Testament: A History* (Philadelphia: Westminster Press, 1983), 266–77.

The emphasis of this passage is on the display of Jesus' power over death, thus a display of his glory; not his glory alone, however (7:18), but also the glory of God working in him. The purpose of this sign, as with the previous signs, is to engender belief in Jesus as one working on behalf of God. This demonstration of his glory should produce belief in Jesus as the one who has come from God. Jesus asks Martha in point-blank fashion, "Do you believe this?" meaning, "Do you believe I am the resurrection and the life?" (v. 27). She responds with a confession of his role as Messiah and Son of God. Similarly, many of the Jews present at the raising of Lazarus also believe in Jesus (v. 45). Martha's response to Jesus before the sign is no more faithful than the Jews' response to him after the sign. In each case, the death and resurrection of Lazarus have presented an opportunity for a response to Jesus. The dramatic delay before he raises Lazarus, followed by the resurrection itself, displays Jesus' nature more vividly than in any of the previous signs—and at the same time crystallizes the responses to him.

The Final Judgment of "the Jews" (11:45–57)

The raising of Lazarus does produce belief among some of "the Jews." But such a response of faith is not universal, even in the face of such a dramatic sign. As has been seen numerous times, "the Jews" are divided in their response (cf. 2:23, 7:30–31, 43–44; 10:19). Some who see the miracle go instead to the Pharisees and chief priests, who assemble a formal council to consider what action may be necessary. Until now, various groups of "Jews" had expressed opposition, often in potentially violent ways. They tried to stone Jesus (8:59; 10:31), to kill him (5:18; 7:1), and to arrest him (7:30, 44; 10:39). But all these were unofficial, spur-of-the-moment reactions. With the raising of Lazarus, however, the actions take on a more official tone with the calling together of the council (the Sanhedrin) to consider formal action.

Again, John's report of the council's action has a paradoxical undertone. The speech of the high priest, Caiaphas, is, on the one hand, a word of misunderstanding. He argues that Jesus should die in order to protect the Jewish nation from retribution by the Romans. On the other hand, the Fourth Evangelist understands the ironic truth to his statement that "it is better for you to have one man die for the people than to have the whole nation destroyed" (v. 50). As the Fourth Evangelist notes, this statement is true—not politically but spiritually, in that through Jesus' death all the children of God might find true life in him. Even in opposition, God's plan in and through Jesus is furthered. The anticipated violent actions are not in opposition to Jesus' role, even though the Sanhedrin is unaware of their complicity in furthering God's revelation of God's glory.

The conclusion of the "trial" by the Sanhedrin is the judgment that Jesus should be put to death. This must be seen as a formal action. In Matthew and Mark, the Sanhedrin takes this action in the final week, after having cross-examined Jesus overnight following his arrest. John's Gospel presents a different scenario. The Fourth Evangelist knows of no trial by the Sanhedrin on the night Jesus was arrested—this had already taken place before the final passion week. And in this early trial as portrayed by John, Jesus is never examined; he is convicted *in absentia*, with no witnesses or charges of criminal behavior. Indeed, the single charge raised, that he performs many signs, is completely true. In presenting the only formal Jewish trial in this fashion, the Fourth Evangelist emphasizes the role "the Jews" play in the final dramatic week. The skirmishes, the attempts to detain and stone Jesus, have all pointed to the coming week. Here the responsibility is laid on the doorstep of the official council. The raising of Lazarus has thus precipitated the coming passion.

? Questions for Reflection

1. What does the reaction of Mary and Martha to the death of Lazarus say about their belief in Jesus?
2. How does Jesus differentiate himself from others who claim to be shepherds?
3. Who/what were the "thieves and bandits" that Jesus was talking about? Who/what are they today?
4. Read John 11:1–16 again. What clues foreshadowing Jesus' own death do you see?

The Final Path to Jerusalem

At the close of chapter 11, the Fourth Gospel signals a chronological shift. The Passover of the Jews has arrived, and the stage is set for a final conflict. We have already seen Jesus' pattern of going to Jerusalem for each of the major feasts, and so the announcement of the Passover sets the stage for a new major conflict between Jesus and "the Jews"—in this case, the passion to come. The narrator builds up the tension by reporting the questioning by the Jews: "Surely he will not come to the festival, will he?" (11:56). The reason for doubting Jesus' attendance, of course, is the arrest warrant that was issued following his kangaroo-court trial. Against this backdrop, the simple announcement in 12:1 that Jesus came to Bethany begins the final drama of Jesus' life.

The Anointing at Bethany (12:1–8)

The arrival at Bethany once again links Jesus to the family of Lazarus, and especially Mary and Martha. The supper setting establishes a close link between Jesus and this family—Lazarus is at the table, Martha serves, and Mary ministers to Jesus. It is interesting that the roles

Mary washing Jesus' feet

77

depicted here are similar to another representation of Mary and Martha, that found in the Gospel of Luke. (See Luke 10:38–41.) The dinner in John's Gospel is the setting for an anointing of Jesus, as well as the first sign of Judas' betrayal.

> "Stories of feet—those of Jesus, anointed by Mary, and those of the disciples, washed by Jesus on the night before his death—have brought us closer to an understanding of Jesus' giving of himself in love for us and the meaning of our own discipleship in obedience to him. Jesus' feet will carry him to a cross, and ours continue to carry us into the world to bear witness to his love."—Gench, *Women and the Word*, 44.

Like Mark and Matthew, John tells the story of a final anointing at Bethany. But in the Fourth Gospel's account, the anointing is significantly different. Here Mary anoints not Jesus' head but rather his feet, with ointment that she then wipes up with her hair. In this description, John is very close to another dinner setting in Luke (7:36–50), in which a sinful woman wipes Jesus' feet with tears and her hair and then anoints his feet with ointment. The similarity of the anointing of the feet and the wiping of them with the hair sets these two accounts apart from the Synoptic accounts in Matthew and Mark. These unique aspects of the anointing must also have struck the Johannine author as important features, for in the raising of Lazarus, Mary is introduced as the one "who anointed the Lord with perfume and wiped his feet with her hair" (11:2), foreshadowing the account found at 12:3.

> "Many have sought to deduce what John means to do by omitting the memorial of Jesus in bread and wine, putting in its place the solicitous deed of washing his disciples' feet. . . . If one is an anti-ritualist, it is easy to say that John inserted an act of personal concern at this point in the narrative to replace a rite which by definition is impersonal. Defenders of the sacrament concept are prone to say that John chose to dwell lovingly on the 'bread come down from heaven' in chapter 6 instead of here."—Sloyan, *John*, Interpretation, 166.

John's account of the anointing has another interesting variant from the Synoptic accounts. In Mark, Jesus answers criticism of the woman's act by responding that she has anointed him for burial in advance of his death (Mark 14:8). John's Gospel, in contrast, has Jesus suggesting that Mary should keep the ointment for the day of burial. Perhaps this reflects another part of the gospel tradition, that women did indeed go to the tomb with spices with which to anoint Jesus after his death (cf. Mark 16:1; Luke 24:1). In both cases, however, Jesus is indicating the nearness of his upcoming death; the anointing is thus the act that introduces the series of passion events.

The dinner scene at Lazarus's house has a dark side as well, for the Fourth Evangelist presents once again the division within Judaism concerning Jesus' actions and his very person. On the one hand, many people come to the house to see Jesus and Lazarus, for the raising of Lazarus has clearly become a major point of interest. Indeed, as the text indicates (12:11), many believe in Jesus because of the raising of Lazarus. But this interest, as has been the pattern throughout the Gospel, causes a counterreaction among other segments of the people. The chief priests, for instance, seek to kill Lazarus as well as Jesus because of the response to Jesus. The dual response of faith by some and attempts to silence Jesus by others—especially by the leaders—is a consistent thread that runs throughout the entire Gospel.

The Triumphal Entry (12:9–19)

In all the Gospels, Jesus enters Jerusalem for a final time in the midst of great festivity. As he enters Jerusalem on a donkey, the crowds welcome him with cries of "Hosanna!" and wave palm branches. But John's version is more explicit in its image of Jesus being received as a king based on a messianic expectation. The following items seem to support the view that this was a royal reception:

1. The crowd adds, at the end of the citation from the Psalms (118:26) in John 12:13, the interpretation "the King of Israel." Thus the crowd is seen to be interpreting the psalm literally as a royal psalm.
2. The riding on the donkey is explicitly interpreted by the evangelist in light of Zechariah 9:9, which indicates that this is how the messianic king will enter Jerusalem.
3. The crowd waves palm branches as Jesus arrives. These branches (the *lulab*) were normally part of the processions at Tabernacles but also were used as an indication of Jewish nationalism. Moreover, the waving of palm branches must have been an intentional and planned act, since palm branches must have been brought up from Jericho or thereabouts. This display of palms on Jesus' entry has explicit messianic overtones.

The entry into Jerusalem is marked by two distinct crowds: one that accompanies Jesus from Bethany and one that greets him in Jerusalem. Once again, those who were present at Lazarus's raising play an important part in this celebration, as they did at Lazarus's house after the anointing. The Fourth Evangelist says that the crowd from Bethany now bears witness to Jesus; John thus links them with another major theme in the Gospel—that of testimony and witness. Just as John the Baptist testified to Jesus and Jesus testifies to the Father, now also the crowd who observed the raising of Lazarus witness to Jesus. But they are met by another crowd who come out because they have heard the witness about the sign of Lazarus. We have, then, in this short scene those who testify (the crowd from Bethany), the object of their testimony (Jesus), and a group who responds to the testimony (the crowd from Jerusalem). This very effective sign of the contagiousness of this early movement is met, however, with a note of skepticism and despair. The Pharisees stand apart from these crowds and complain, prophetically, that the "world has gone after him." This saying by the Pharisees highlights another theme in the Fourth Gospel—the reaction of the "world" to Jesus, a reaction that is mixed at best.

> "Modern acquisitive life is a matter of 'hanging on.' Being told to follow the injunction of Jesus, to let go, to die, to go into the earth so as to bear much fruit, creates consternation. Those who see in it the germ of a counsel for the good of nations have to be laughed out of court. Imagine a world without cutthroat economic competition, without the profit motive as the highest motive. To lose selfhood through losing the possessions that define selfhood is not the world's way."—Sloyan, *John,* Interpretation, 157.

> "The promise of glory is the promise, almost incredible and only possible by the work of Christ, that some of us, that any of us who really chooses, shall actually survive that examination, shall find approval, shall please God. To please God . . . to be a real ingredient in the divine happiness . . . to be loved by God, not merely pitied, but delighted in as an artist delights in his work or a father in a son—it seems impossible, a weight or burden of glory which our thoughts can hardly sustain. But so it is."—C. S. Lewis, from "The Weight of Glory," quoted in *The Westminster Dictionary of Christian Meditations* (Louisville, Ky.: Westminster John Knox Press, 2000), 415.

Jesus' Sayings before the Passion (12:20–36)

As if to amplify the Pharisees' statement, the evangelist introduces a curious episode in which some Greeks present at the Passover seek Jesus. Are these examples of "the world"? It would seem in the context of the passage that this is so. But it is perhaps too much of a leap to assume that these Greeks are Gentiles. If they were, why would they be in Jerusalem to worship? Rather, they appear to be Greek-speaking Jews who are present for the Passover feast (cf. Acts 2:1–13 for the example of foreign Jews coming to Jerusalem on feast days). But this incident still makes the testimony about Jesus of worldwide importance, not just for Palestine.

In response to the Greeks' request to see him, Jesus instead announces that the passion is upon them: "The hour has come for the Son of Man to be glorified." John frequently uses the word *hour* to speak of the focal event of the Gospel—the crucifixion of Jesus. This central moment was anticipated as early as 2:4, when Jesus responded to his mother that his hour had not yet come. At various points in the Gospel, the future event is obliquely referred to as the "hour": at 5:25, 27, Jesus speaks of the hour when the dead will hear the voice of the Son of God; 7:30 and 8:20, where the Jews are unable to capture him, also contains a reference to "his hour"—it was because his "hour" had not yet come that the potential captors were unsuccessful. And after Jesus' announcement in 12:23, 27 that the hour has indeed arrived, he uses this term at key points to refer to his coming death (13:1; 17:1). The term gives a sense of fixity to the events that follow; they are part of a preconceived plan of which only Jesus and his Father are aware.

Jesus uses the term *glorified* to refer to the passion, and this also is a theologically important word. For Jesus, the death and resurrection will allow his glory as the Son of God to become manifest, and through it, God will be given glory. At the very beginning of the Gospel (1:14), Jesus' manifestation in the flesh was said to be "glory," the glory of the only Son of the Father. So, similarly, at his first sign at Cana he showed his "glory." And at certain key points in the narrative, the evangelist uses the term *glorified* to speak of Jesus' death and resurrection (7:39; 11:4; 12:16). This use of the term by Jesus himself to speak of his death, however, anticipates a frequent use of the "glorification" in the Gospel. As we shall see, the concept of glorification is a central part of how Jesus understands his coming death. For this reason, chapters 13–20 have often been called "The Book of Glory."

The importance of the term is seen most clearly in Jesus' own cry to God: "Father glorify your name" (12:28). Only at this point in the Fourth Gospel does God audibly speak, since John reports no voice from heaven at the baptism, nor does the Fourth Gospel contain an account of a transfiguration where God speaks from the clouds. God's words, "I have glorified it, and I will glorify it again," speak to the importance of this idea in John's understanding of the crucifixion and resurrection. Notice also that Jesus and God are speaking about the glorification of God's name, not of Jesus. Glorification of Jesus is always a glorification of God. At numerous points, Jesus goes to great lengths to point away from himself and toward God as the proper object of glory or the only true source of glory (8:54; 13:31; 14:13; 17:1–5).

Jesus' prayer to God to glorify God's name through Jesus' death comes in the context of a personal dedication to the task at hand. In contrast to the other Gospels, which have Jesus praying fervently in the garden before his arrest, the unit of 12:27–36 is the closest John comes to indicating Jesus' own turmoil at the prospect of dying. "Now my soul is troubled. And what should I say—'Father, save me from this hour'? No, it is for this reason that I have come to this hour" (12:27). Jesus faces his own fears at the prospect of the crucifixion and yet is resolute because he knows that is why he has been sent. The Fourth Gospel consistently shows Jesus as knowing his fate and facing it with resolve. And this attitude is particularly appropriate for John's image of Jesus, who, as the Word of God come into the world, remains in constant communication with God. But even with this consistent portrayal of Jesus as intimately involved in God's purpose, John also shows that he is human, with human fears.

That Jesus' death is imminent becomes obvious from the rest of the discourse in this section. Jesus uses two images to describe his death, that of the seed falling to the earth (12:24) and that of being "lifted up"(12:32). The latter is explicitly said by the Fourth Evangelist to refer to the crucifixion and also seems to recall Jesus' statement in 3:14, in which he compared being lifted up to Moses lifting up the bronze snake on his staff in order to provide healing for the people. In both instances, Jesus argues that his death will bring salvation for those who believe. The dying wheat grain bears much fruit; in being lifted up, Jesus will draw all humanity to him.

A Summary Assessment (12:37–50)

After Jesus' prayer and teaching about his coming passion, Jesus is said to have hidden from the Jews. It is not actually clear whom he is hiding from—the crowds or the Pharisees. But the narrator interprets all of this in terms of "the Jews," for he says that "they" did not believe in Jesus. The term *the Jews* has been used to describe those in Judaism who have refused to believe in Jesus and his mission. (See page 5.) Again in this section, we find a tension between belief and unbelief. In the preceding passages, many followed Jesus from Lazarus's house because he had performed the sign of raising from the dead, and many more came out to greet Jesus at his entry into Jerusalem because of the witness others gave about his signs. Furthermore, in 12:42, the Fourth Evangelist wants the reader to know that many of the "authorities" believed in Jesus yet did not openly confess it for fear of being cast out of the synagogue (an echo of the response of the blind man's parents in 9:22). So, in this final narrative before the passion proper, there are some who believe. Yet there are those who do not. This has been the pattern throughout the Gospel, from the first sign at Cana to the present.

How does John explain this radical difference in the reception of Jesus? This stubborn lack of belief, even in the face of signs, must have its origination in God's own plan. Drawing on two passages from Isaiah (Isa. 53:1; 6:10), John explains this as a divine hardening of the heart. It is interesting that the latter Isaiah passage is used as well by the Synoptic Gospels to refer to the inability of people to interpret the parables (Matt. 13:14; Mark 4:12; Luke 8:10). Such a hardening of the heart must be God's judgment on a people who have refused to listen to God's teachings, so that even in the face of signs and teachings they choose to oppose the living Word of God.

John adds a final discourse by Jesus that further amplifies the importance of the division in the Jews' response to Jesus. The choice between believing and not believing in Jesus and his words is ultimately a choice about God, not just about Jesus. Believing in Jesus involves

> "Betrayal and denial are never far, even for those who have witnessed the signs, heard the Word, and participated in his service."

recognizing the true nature of God, who sent him. Jesus was sent as light to the world for the purpose of redemption and salvation. In following Jesus, the believer is actually following the commandments of God. At the same time, refusal to believe will bring about judgment for ignoring God's commands. This choice, then, is crucial. It is the central choice, the central "crisis," that runs throughout the Gospel.

The Final Supper (13:1–20)

In all the Gospels, Jesus celebrates a final supper with his disciples on Thursday night before his crucifixion. John's depiction of this supper is significantly different in a number ways: in the date relative to the Passover feast, in the absence of eucharistic language, and in the presence of the footwashing. Moreover, John interprets Judas in a slightly different light from the other Gospels.

While the final supper in John is on Thursday night, unlike the other Gospels this is not the night of the Passover feast but rather the evening before. In all the Synoptic Gospels, the final meal on Thursday evening is a Passover meal, the first night of the Feast of Passover and Unleavened Bread. On this day the Passover lamb was sacrificed in the Temple and then cooked and eaten before sunrise the next day. At the meal, the exodus from Egypt was remembered. The Passover meal involved a number of ritual passages from scripture, told between blessings and cups of wine. This formal meal, which needed to be set up in advance, fits well with the descriptions in the Synoptic Gospels.

The Last Supper in the Four Gospels

There are several significant differences between John's account of the Last Supper and the Synoptic accounts: in the date relative to the Passover feast, in the presence of the footwashing, in the portrayal of Judas, and in the absence in John of eucharistic language for the meal. For the Synoptic Gospel accounts of the Last Supper, read Matthew 26:17–29; Mark 14:17–25; and Luke 22:14–23.

John, by contrast, makes it clear that the final meal was not a Passover meal. There is no mention of any preparation for the meal, the securing of an upper room, or any of the other indications of a special gathering. Moreover, when Jesus is tried before Pilate the next day (Friday), the Jewish accusers will not enter into Pilate's palace because they do not want to make themselves impure. This, John notes, is because they had not yet eaten the Passover (18:28). John's dating relative to the Jewish calendar is, therefore, different from that in the Synoptics.

How might one explain the difference between John and the other Gospels? One explanation is a theological tendency on the part of either John or the Synoptics. It is possible that, given the closeness to the Passover, Mark may have assumed the final dinner was a Passover meal and so interpreted the event. The Passover meal would provide a perfect opportunity to explain the Eucharist, with its breaking of bread and drinking of wine. In contrast, many have argued that John may have wanted to modify his account so that Jesus is actually crucified at the same time the Passover lamb was being slaughtered in the temple. This would fit with John the Baptist's designation of Jesus as "the Lamb of God who takes away the sin of the world" (1:29). But if this was a deliberate modification by the Fourth Evangelist, it is a bit curious too, for the evangelist never makes explicit at Jesus' crucifixion that Jesus is the Lamb of God, the Passover lamb. Moreover, the Passover lamb was not considered an atoning sacrifice (i.e., it did not remove sin) but was rather part of a feast of remembrance.

It has been carefully argued that John's depiction of the day on which Passover was observed (Friday, not Thursday) fits more accurately the situation during the most likely years of Jesus' death. (See J. A. T. Robinson, *The Priority of John*, 153.) Finally, some have seen a possible explanation in the difference between the calendar followed by the Pharisees and Sadducees (the current Jewish lunar calendar) and the calendar of the Essenes (a solar calendar).

There is no obvious solution to the problem of the difference in dating between John's final supper and the Lord's Supper of the Synoptic Gospels. Most likely, John and the Synoptics derive from independent oral traditions. But John's dating explains, in part, the absence of the eucharistic language—language that is instead found in Jesus' discourse at the feeding of the five thousand (6:48–59). Likewise, the Synoptic placement at the Passover meal may well explain the Lord's Supper language there.

Equally striking, however, is the Fourth Gospel's portrayal of the footwashing. Instead of words spoken over the meal (as in the Synoptic Gospels' Lord's Supper), the central focus of this final meal is found in Jesus' action toward his disciples. He assumes the posture of a servant; taking a towel and a basin, he washes his disciples' feet. It is not clear how prevalent footwashing was in antiquity. Most likely, guests would wash their own feet on arrival for a dinner. There is some evidence at least that providing a basin for footwashing was a sign of hospitality (cf. Luke 7:44). But John's portrayal is especially unusual since it has Jesus washing his disciples' feet *during* the dinner, not before it. This placement surely is meant to amplify the act's importance and to give it greater meaning.

It is the servant role that is clearly at issue. In a final interpretation of this action, Jesus makes it clear that he is teaching them how to act with one another and, by extension, demonstrating how all Christians are to act with one another:

> Do you know what I have done to you? You call me Teacher and Lord—and you are right, for that is what I am. So if I, your Lord and Teacher, have washed your feet, you also ought to wash one another's feet. For I have set you an example, that you also should do as I have done to you. (13:12–15)

A key question the church must face is whether this example is to be interpreted literally, as a sacrament of footwashing, or figuratively, as simply an instruction on an appropriate servant posture. Few churches have taken the command literally, although some have. In the early church, we have some evidence that footwashing was a religious act; 1 Timothy 5:10 lists this as an act of piety that demonstrates acceptability to be enrolled as a widow. But this passage in 1 Timothy may only refer to traditional acts of hospitality by those of lesser rank (women); it does not speak to the radical nature of servanthood that John is describing. Certainly, servanthood is a central part of Jesus' teaching. The idea that the greatest should be least is woven through many of the Gospels (cf. Mark 10:43–44; and note the addition in Luke 22:25–27, that Jesus has given an example of service at the table). This would imply that service toward those of lower stature, whether social or economic, is an essential part of the command to love one another, a commandment that is made more explicit in the subsequent dialogue.

The footwashing episode contains a note of resistance, however. Peter at first resists the need for footwashing, perhaps because he cannot accept the reversal of roles that Jesus' washing of feet involves. But Jesus is adamant—unless Peter lets his feet be washed, he can have no part in Jesus. This is a strong statement, suggesting that failure to participate will put Peter outside a functional relationship, outside the church. Peter then reverses course and wants to be washed all over, an overreaction that Jesus also rebuffs.

Up to this point in the Gospel, Peter has been a minor character. Aside from joining Jesus at the beginning of the Gospel, Peter emerged only at the conclusion of the feeding of the five thousand, when he gave something similar to a confession that Jesus is Lord. But here and in subsequent scenes in the passion and resurrection story, Peter's character becomes more fully developed. In this footwashing account, we see Peter's rash and impetuous character, as it is commonly depicted in the Synoptic Gospels. He misunderstands the purpose of the footwashing, reacts negatively at first, and then oversteps in an attempt to correct his initial mistake. As in the other Gospels, Peter serves in the Fourth Gospel as a contrast to Jesus—while well meaning, he often reaches the wrong decisions and acts before he thinks.

Predictions of Betrayal and Denial (13:21–38)

The figure of Judas Iscariot particularly stands out in John's narration of the story of Jesus. As in all the Gospels, Judas is the disciple who betrays Jesus and leads the Jewish leaders to him after the supper. But John has two narrative details that make Judas a striking figure in the developing story: the depiction of Satan's role in Judas's betrayal and the details of the prediction of betrayal at the final supper.

John says two times in the story of the final supper that Satan "entered into" Judas. The first of these announcements is found in the introductory sentence to the footwashing. Before describing the footwashing, the narrator informs the reader that "the devil" (the slanderer, *diabolos*) had already put the idea of betrayal into Judas's heart. This information is related along with the fact that Jesus knew God's intention and his own origination from God. Then, after the supper with the disciples, the reader learns that Satan (the accuser, *Satanas*) has "entered into" Judas, whereupon Judas departs from the dinner to betray Jesus. These two references to a sinister spiritual cause underlying Judas's betrayal frame Jesus' prediction of that betrayal, and they accentuate the importance of Jesus' upcoming death as one involving a spiritual choice between good and evil, between God and the devil. It appears that at the very moment Jesus is completely aware of his fate, his origination, and his destination, we also learn of spiritual opponents to Jesus.

The Last Supper

In addition to these two references, John has prepared the reader for the betrayal and its attribution to the devil early on in the Gospel. In 6:70, after Peter's "good confession," Jesus says, "Did I not choose you, the twelve? Yet one of you is a devil." The narrator then informs us that Jesus was speaking of

Want to Know More?

About Passover? See Paul J. Achtemeier, ed., *HarperCollins Bible Dictionary*, rev. ed. (New York: HarperCollins, 1996), 810–12.

Judas Iscariot. This feature of Judas's relationship to the devil/Satan is important to the Fourth Gospel. Moreover, this theme of the diabolical nature of Judas's betrayal is closely linked in the narrative with passages about Peter. Where this depiction of Judas is reported, Peter is first presented as a positive disciple, followed by Judas as a negative disciple.

But John is not the only Gospel writer to suggest that Judas was under the influence of Satan. Luke also says, just before the Lord's Supper, that "Satan entered into Judas called Iscariot" (Luke 22:3), echoing closely the language of the Fourth Gospel. It is unlikely that John learned of this interpretation of Judas's actions from Luke; while this feature is found only briefly in Luke, it is woven into John's account in a number of places and seems to fit well with John's dualistic view of the universe—a universe marked by the stark choice between good and evil, light and dark. More likely, Luke borrowed the idea from either John's Gospel or a common tradition.

The story leading up to Judas's betrayal is also noteworthy because of how John describes the final supper. At that supper, Jesus clearly already knows that Judas will betray him. We learn this first at John 6:71, and during the supper Jesus announces openly to all the disciples that "one of you will betray me." When asked by the beloved disciple who the betrayer is, Jesus says it will be the one to whom he gives the morsel of bread dipped in the wine. Jesus, then, knows Judas as the betrayer, yet they share this final meal together. Indeed, Jesus appears to be complicit in the act of betrayal, for after giving the bread to Judas, he bids him, "Do quickly what you are going to do" (13:28). Judas, by participating in the dinner with Jesus and apparently having his feet washed by Jesus as well, is a very intimate betrayer. And Jesus is aware not only of the fact of his betrayal but also of which person will betray him. Thus Judas is linked even more closely with Jesus' intimates, as part of the inner circle; his betrayal, therefore, is both a violation of close friendship and a sign of a deeper spiritual battle.

The closing verse of the dinner scene aptly summarizes the spiritual emphasis of the betrayal. On receiving the morsel, Judas immediately goes out. And then, the evangelist tells us, "it was night." This final verse, so simple and stark, returns to the darkness/light motif with which John began his Gospel. Jesus is the light of the world, come into a dark world. Judas, in rejecting Jesus, has turned his back on the light and reentered the dark. The fact that he goes into the night serves to punctuate the spiritual choice Judas has made.

After Judas's departure, Jesus gives a final teaching that in many ways serves as a contrast to Judas's action. Predicting his own death as his departure from his disciples, Jesus summarizes the ethic of the new kingdom: love one another. He calls this a new commandment and uses his actions with the disciples as an example of what this love should look like. Moreover, this love for one another is to be the distinguishing characteristic of the true disciples of Jesus. But the backdrop of this commandment is the knowledge that one of the disciples has already turned his back on true discipleship, choosing instead to betray Jesus to the Jewish authorities.

Given both Jesus' commandment of love and Judas's impending betrayal under the impetus of Satan, the subsequent portrayal of Peter underlines his character as rash and impetuous and further serves as a warning to all disciples, present and future, about the tenuous nature of discipleship. When Jesus says that where he is going they cannot come (meaning death by crucifixion and then heaven), Peter rashly asserts that he is willing to lay his life down for Jesus. But, as in all the Gospels, Jesus predicts that Peter will instead deny him three times. Peter's intentions again exceed his ability or his knowledge.

Peter and Judas become important characters for the developing story of Jesus and important types for all followers of Jesus. Even as Jesus is urging the disciples to love and to serve, one of them turns his back completely on the truth, while another makes rash statements that betray a weakness of character. Even among the closest followers of Jesus, who believed at the beginning of the story (2:11) and did not depart from him, are those who are close to disbelief. Betrayal and denial are never far, even for those who have witnessed the signs, heard the Word, and participated in his service.

❓ Questions for Reflection

1. Have you ever participated in a footwashing service? Describe the experience.
2. The raising of Lazarus prompted belief in some but a strong desire to kill Jesus and Lazarus in others. Why do you think reactions were so different?
3. The Pharisees complained that "the world" had "gone after" Jesus. What did they mean by that? Who was "the world?"
4. John is the only one of the Gospels not to incorporate eucharistic language into the passage on the Last Supper. Do you think this was deliberate on the Gospel writer's account? Why or why not?

8 John 14–17

The Farewell Sayings

The Gospel of John has a distinctive structure: a narrative about Jesus and his signs that is periodically interspersed with long dialogues or discourses. Some of these have already been noted in the previous units. For instance, in his discussion with Nicodemus, Jesus answers Nicodemus's queries in relatively long responses. After the feeding of the five thousand (John 6) and again after the Tabernacles controversies (John 10), John portrays Jesus giving long discourses about his nature. Many of these discourses involve "I am" sayings, in which Jesus echoes God's self-revealing name ("I am who I am") to disclose his own divine nature to the disciples and other audiences. After the final supper, though, the evangelist presents a long block of discourses that are self-revelatory in nature and also serve as a farewell to the disciples. Chapters 14–17 are presented as almost a continuous block of Jesus' teaching, broken only by small responses by the disciples at 14:4–8, 22 and 16:17–18, 29–30.

There is no apparent structure to the discourses that have been gathered together in chapters 14–17. Many times the same themes recur in variations (e.g., the anticipation of the Paraclete, teaching about "abiding" in Jesus), creating a sense of overlapping ideas and often echoing themes that have appeared in the preceding narrative leading up to the passion. It is worthwhile, then, to consider this long block of discourses thematically, not in the order in which they appear.

Jesus' Departure and His Promise

Jesus begins his long series of discourses in the form of a farewell speech. He has previously announced to both the Jews (7:33) and the disciples (13:33) that he is "going away," indeed to a place where they cannot follow immediately, and the beginning of his farewell speech develops this idea more fully. Jesus says that he is going away but that this departure is actually good news, for he will prepare a place for them and await them there (14:1–4). This place is with the Father— that is, in God's dwelling place.

The departure theme is picked up in a number of places and serves as the thread that binds the entire discourse together. Jesus is leaving, but his departure will allow the Paraclete to come (14:18). This departure is good news, since Jesus goes to God (14:28). Now is the time that Jesus must depart, to return to the one who sent him (16:5). And the departure motif becomes an assumed feature in Jesus' final prayer, chapter 17, where the use of the past tense assumes his life is over, and he is reflecting on the effect he will have on his followers.

In John's opening Prologue, a clear spatial metaphor is used to describe the relationship between the realm of God and the realm of humanity. These two realms are seen as "places" between which travel is possible. Thus Jesus was "coming into the world" from the realm of God (1:9). And in the dialogue with Nicodemus, Jesus spoke of this entry as a descent— "No one has ascended into heaven except the one who descended from heaven, the Son of Man" (3:13). This spatial metaphor of heaven as a place

> "Jesus himself is the route, the underlying reason for the journey. He is way and truth and life. . . . He alone is the way to the Father. All approach to God is through him."—Sloyan, *John,* Interpretation, 179.

"up there" to which Jesus will return pervades his departure sayings. He will go to that place to prepare an abiding place ("mansions" in the King James version) for the believers. Just as he left the realm of God in order to come into the world, so he will now leave the world to return to God (16:28). So, likewise, when he prays to God, he looks up to heaven (17:1) as an indication of the place where God is and to which Jesus will return.

This spatial separation, then, is assumed in the various departure references, especially the opening verses of chapter 14. Jesus is "going away" to prepare a place, but he will come back and accompany the believers on the journey to this place. But at another level, Jesus also refutes the spatial sense. When Philip asks him to show the disciples the Father—a question that seems to be requesting that Jesus show the way to this place where God is—Jesus' response turns the spatial metaphor on its head. Jesus has already shown the Father to them in his own person. God's place is already with them, for God dwells in Jesus and Jesus is dwelling with them.

The spatial metaphor is modified as well in a key verse in chapter 14. In response to Thomas's question, "How can we know the way?" Jesus says, "I am the way, and the truth, and the life. No one comes to the Father except through me" (14:6). Here Jesus expands and interprets further the spatial concept. Not only is there a place to which Jesus will go and to which he will also bring all believers, but the pathway between "the world" and "heaven" is Jesus himself. Thus Jesus also becomes a part of this spiritual geography. Although occurring only as a single verse here, this is a key concept in John throughout. Jesus is not just any messenger from God; he is the messenger who uniquely exhibits God's nature and design and who alone can connect humanity with the God whom they have rejected and ignored.

> "I am the way, and the truth, and the life. No one comes to the Father except through me" (John 14:6).

Jesus' departure is consistently framed as a promise of future benefits. He goes away in order to prepare a place for believers (14:2). Jesus' departure will allow for a future reunion, which will be a cause for joy (16:22). His departure will also allow the coming of the Paraclete, who will strengthen and guide the disciples (14:15; 15:26). Moreover, Jesus' departure will allow the disciples to do works in his name, works that can be requested in his name in order to further the glorification of God in Jesus. This theme is emphasized twice, first in 14:12 and subsequently in 16:23–24. The believer will receive the ability to ask of God directly and is promised to receive gifts from God. While the passage in 16:23–24 is fairly open-ended ("if you ask anything of the Father in my name, he will give it to you"), the first mention of this promise of answered prayer seems to be in the context of ministry—of doing the works that will further glorify God in the name of Jesus.

The departure of Jesus is described not only in spatial terms but also in chronological terms. Jesus is said to go away for a time, and after a while he will return (16:16). But the emphasis on time is also used to impress on the disciples the immediate urgency of the departure. The time of his departure is but a "little time." In other words, the hour of his crucifixion lies just around the corner, and so all that he is discussing is immediate. Again, John's Gospel uses the distinctive term *the hour* in ways that are meaningful yet mundane. On the one hand, "the hour" seems to refer simply to the future—"The hour is coming when I will no longer speak to you in figures" (16:25). On the other hand, it seems to carry with it all the theological meaning of the crucial moment when Jesus is glorified—the crucifixion, at which Jesus truly shows that he and God are one (16:32).

The Paraclete

A key promise that Jesus makes in discussing his departure is that the Paraclete will come and will assist the believers in Jesus' absence. The coming Paraclete is a striking feature of the farewell discourses.

Parakletos has been translated in various ways: counselor, advocate, comforter, helper. Literally, it means one who is called to the aid of another. Outside the New Testament, the term was used for a legal assistant or advocate, a slave who was called to assist, and an intercessor in legal or administrative difficulties. John's language makes it clear that this Paraclete will come as an assistant to aid the believers in a number of important matters. The Paraclete will teach the disciples (14:26; 16:13) and will remind

> "The word *parakalein* is the word for exhorting men to noble deeds and high thoughts; it is especially the word of courage before battle. Life is always calling us into battle and the one who makes us able to stand up to the opposing forces, to cope with life and to conquer life is the *parakletos*, the Holy Spirit, who is none other than the presence and the power of the risen Christ."—Barclay, *New Testament Words*, 222.

them of what Jesus said while he was alive (14:26). It will provide testimony on behalf of Jesus, perhaps aiding the disciples in their own testimony on behalf of Jesus (15:26–27).

The Paraclete is plainly identified as the Holy Spirit (14:26) and also as the "Spirit of truth" (15:26; 16:13). It will be sent from God at Jesus' request and clearly is to be sent as an aid for the believers forever (14:16). The Holy Spirit will be a known presence among the disciples but will not be readily apparent to the world. It is, then, a spiritual presence for believers and is thus closely connected with Jesus himself. Just as the disciples are to abide in Jesus and Jesus will abide in them, so also the Holy Spirit is said to abide with the disciples (14:16). As appears in the apostle Paul's language about the Holy Spirit, it is more probable that the Holy Spirit is to dwell in the community of believers than in individual Christians. The language "it will abide (or dwell) in you" should be better translated "it will abide (or dwell) among you." But either way, the Paraclete, the Holy Spirit, is to be a sign of Jesus' continuing presence in the world. In this sense, then, Jesus can say he will not leave the disciples orphaned—for in the Paraclete, Jesus will simultaneously abide among the believers even as he abides in God.

Jesus prays

The importance of this promise of the Paraclete can be seen in the postresurrection scene with the disciples. When they understand that Jesus has risen and is standing in their midst, he breathes on them and says, "Receive the Holy Spirit" (20:22). Here, then, the promise made in the farewell discourses is fulfilled at the resurrection of Jesus as he is ready to ascend to God.

Abide in Me

A strong theme in the farewell discourses is the need for the followers of Jesus to abide or remain in Jesus even after his departure. In many ways, this "abiding" (Greek, *meno*) is seen as one of the key ways in which belief and love are manifested. Indeed, these terms—*abide, believe,* and *love*—seem at times to be variants of the same concept.

Jesus in this Gospel has already sounded the theme of "abiding" in terms of the believers continuing the relationship with him. In 8:31, Jesus defined discipleship in terms of abiding in his word: "If you continue [abide] in my word, you are truly my disciples; and you will know the truth, and the truth will make you free." But this saying became a point of contention because the Jewish "believers" could not accept the idea that they were under bondage. The resulting conflict over Jesus' relationship to Abraham demonstrated that their belief was not solid. What Jesus was indicating at this point was the close relationship between belief and abiding in Jesus' words as a total approach to life. For Jesus, belief implies a foundational relationship that informs all other actions.

It is precisely this kind of an understanding of "abiding" that we begin to see in the first part of the farewell dialogue. In 14:10, when asked to show the disciples the Father, Jesus indicates that the Father has been abiding in Jesus throughout his ministry and that this close relationship is what has allowed Jesus to speak with authority and act with power. Thus, Jesus' own relationship with God is defined in terms of "abiding," a term that is further developed later on. More-

over, Jesus' own abiding with God is to be extended to the disciples—
"On that day you will know that I am in my Father, and you in me,
and I in you" (14:20).

In chapter 15, Jesus picks up this theme of "abiding in him" and
develops it as a major unit of the farewell discourse. Using the
metaphor of the grapevine, Jesus suggests that the disciples are to have
the kind of close relationship with him that branches of the grapevine
have with the main stem. The branches are unable to be fruitful, to
even exist, without being connected to the vine. It is precisely this
kind of close relationship that Jesus goes on to define as "abiding" in
him. Each is to remain or abide in the other—the disciples are to
abide in Jesus, and in the same way Jesus will abide with the disciples,
in their very midst, as a continuing presence. In many ways, this abiding presumes the power and presence of the Paraclete, but it remains
a powerful statement of Jesus' own close relationship with his disciples and all who believe in him.

The concept of abiding is further defined in a number of key ways,
though these are not independent definitions but rather are all part
of the same fundamental reality. Notice how Jesus' argument about
abiding in him progresses:

1. "Bear much fruit and become my disciples" (15:8). Playing off
   the initial metaphor of the vine and the branches, Jesus defines
   discipleship in terms of its results. To be a disciple is a matter
   not just of believing in some sterile way but of demonstrating
   that belief in tangible, productive ways. By linking discipleship
   to tangible results, Jesus sounds a theme similar to that found
   in chapter 8, where he directs the believers to abide in his word.
2. "Abide in my love" (15:9). Fundamentally, abiding in Jesus
   means to remain tied to the very nature of Jesus, who loved the
   world and loved his disciples. Thus, being a disciple means to
   remain rooted in the very nature of Jesus' mission—to love the
   world and so bring light into darkness.
3. "If you keep my commandments, you will abide in my love"
   (15:10). But abiding in Jesus' love is not a matter of belief or
   emotion; it is ultimately proven by action. So keeping his commandments is the basis for proving that one abides in that love.
   Earlier, in 14:15, Jesus affirmed the connection between keeping his commandments and loving him. Indeed, Jesus said that
   following God's commandments is how he demonstrates his
   own love for God: "I do as the Father has commanded me, so

that the world may know that I love the Father" (14:31). In chapter 15, Jesus returns to the connection between keeping commandments and love. The two are inextricably linked—one cannot truly love God without following God's wishes. In the same way, one cannot truly say he or she abides in Jesus' love without following his wishes, which are the same as God's.

4. "This is my commandment, that you love one another" (15:12). This commandment to love one another was first explicitly introduced in the final scenes of the supper (13:34). It was repeated at 14:21. In this context, Jesus links the commandment to love one another with the desire to remain in his love. In other words, one cannot love Jesus without manifesting that same love toward others. Here is the core of Jesus' self-revelation: self-giving love.

> "Jesus is the vine of the church, out of, into, and around which all the branches grow. The vine metaphor is a powerful image of the church: the center vine out of which the branches grow is identifiable, but the mass of intertwining branches is indistinguishable. . . . Hierarchy among members is impossible in the vine of the church, because all members grow out of the same vine and are tended equally by the one vine grower."—Gail O'Day, in Newsom and Ringe, eds., *Women's Bible Commentary*, 392.

The intimate relationship between Jesus and his disciples that is implied in the term *abide* finds a final expression at the close of Jesus' prayer in chapter 17. There, Jesus petitions God that the same intimate relationship he has with his Father be present between him and his disciples as well (see 17:22–24). While the word *abide* is not present in this verse, the concept that Jesus developed earlier is fully present. Abiding is intimately linked to love, to proving discipleship, to loving one another.

The Love Commandment

As noted in the discussion about the final supper, as well as in the discussion about the phrase "abide with me," Jesus' command to love one another is a bold and striking element in his final instructions to his disciples. This explicit commandment is found in 15:12 as well as 13:34. But this commandment is linked to a broader theme that runs through the entire Gospel, and especially through the discourses in chapters 14–17: the understanding that Jesus' mission is to be comprehended as God's love for humanity and that humans are to respond in a similar way.

In 15:12–17, Jesus focuses attention on the importance of this commandment. The disciples are to love one another in the same way that Jesus has already loved them. Jesus, then, is the example par excellence of love. In this statement is comprehended the entire ministry up to this point. Within the Gospel of John, this includes the close association Jesus has had with his disciples, his acts of healing, his attitude of healing, and his showing God's nature to them. But the statement "as I have loved you" also points forward to the next statement about the willingness to lay down one's life for friends. Jesus himself is in the process of laying down his life on behalf of the entire world, and this self-sacrificing attitude is to be the hallmark of love.

Jesus introduces the word *friend* into the equation at this point (15:13). The one who is truly a friend to others is willing to lay down one's life for one's friends. Jesus then defines his relationship with the disciples as "friends," as opposed to a "master-servant" relationship. As friends, Jesus has included them in his plans and has revealed his nature and his future. There is a relationship of intimacy drawn here: Jesus personally chose these disciples, included them in his closest counsel, and cared for them in a special way—the way of friendship. But friendship is reciprocal, and the disciples will demonstrate that they, too, are friends, by following Jesus' commandment to love one another. As friends, therefore, they are to pattern their life for one another on his example as the friend who demonstrates the greatest love.

The linkage of loving Jesus and keeping his commandments has already been introduced in these farewell discourses (see 14:15–31). This demonstration of love by the followers of Jesus will bring them into the circle of love already experienced by Jesus and God. Thus love, by both disciples and Jesus, is reciprocal: the disciples are to reciprocate Jesus' love by keeping his commandment, and Jesus and God reciprocate their love by bringing the disciples into the circle of divine love and making their home with them (14:23).

The theme of love has been raised a number of times in the Fourth Gospel, so these discourses only amplify a concept that has been shown before in Jesus' ministry. Jesus' well-known statement in 3:16—"God so loved the world that he gave his only Son, so that everyone who believes in him may not perish but may have eternal life"—rightly stands out because it captures John's understanding of Jesus' mission so well. God's attitude toward humanity is love. And God demonstrates that, first and foremost, by loving the Son and placing all things in his hands (3:35). A test of whether someone truly knows God is seen in how he or she responds to Jesus; those who do not love Jesus also do not really know God (8:42). That this theme is central to John's presentation of Jesus' mission is clearly seen in the opening verse of the passion narrative: "Having loved his own who were in the world, he loved them to the end" (13:1). The command to love one another is a way of making this central concept in Jesus' mission tangible for the disciples as Jesus prepares for his death.

Unity among Believers

Related to the concepts of remaining (abiding) in Jesus and loving one another is the idea of Christian unity. This is brought to beautiful expression in the final chapter of the farewell discourse, commonly called Jesus' "high-priestly prayer." In chapter 17, Jesus does not speak directly to the disciples but rather allows them to overhear his prayer to God.

> "The glory that you have given me I have given them, so that they may be one, as we are one, I in them and you in me, that they may become completely one, so that the world may know that you have sent me and have loved them even as you have loved me'" (John 17:22–23).

In the conclusion of Jesus' prayer, he asks that all his followers should be unified. The example for that unity is the relationship that Jesus has with God—they are one, so also believers should be one (17:22). This unity among believers is to be a demonstration of God's love for Jesus and therefore for the world. And unity among believers is to demonstrate how God and Jesus continue to abide in the community of believers: " . . . so that they may be one, as we are one, I in them and you in me, that they may become completely one, so that the world may know that you have sent me and have loved them even as you have loved me" (17:22–23). In this prayer for unity, then, the key themes of abiding in Jesus and love are shown to be integrally related concepts.

The Importance of Belief in Jesus

Throughout the Gospel, a key issue has been belief. The Prologue pronounces that John the Baptist's mission was to testify in order that all might believe in Jesus (1:7). When Jesus performed signs and taught, a division ensued: some believed, others did not (see 2:11, 23; 4:53; 6:66; 9:37; 11:45–46). Belief in Jesus will result in life, disbelief in death (5:24). The entire purpose of Jesus' ministry is that people should believe in him as the one sent from God; this response of faith defines the only acceptable posture that humanity can have toward God (5:46; 6:29) and indeed offers believers the power to become the children of God (1:12).

This theme of belief is also central in the final discourses. The opening verse of the discourse, 14:1, puts it as an entreaty or command: "Believe in God, believe also in me." Here is the core message of the Gospel: to know and believe in God is to believe in Jesus. And to know and believe in Jesus is to truly know God. One who wants to know God need only know Jesus as the true image of God. "Whoever has seen me has seen the Father. How can you say, 'Show us the Father'? Do you not believe that I am in the Father and the Father is in me?" (14:9–10).

> "Do preachers regularly invite their congregants to anything like the high standard of John 17? Whether they do or not, they should. . . . This possession of eternal life should be preached, but in a state of awe that the Evangelist and his company did so know God, and in hope that preacher and hearer may do the same."—Sloyan, *John,* Interpretation, 199.

For those who believe, the relationship with God is secure and has a future. God loves those who have come to believe in Jesus as the one sent from God (16:27). It is these followers who have believed in Jesus, and who thus truly understand God's nature, for whom Jesus prays (17:8, 20), and it is for the purpose of bringing about belief in the world that he entreats unity (17:21). By the same token, however, those who disbelieve are counted as outsiders to the promises. Jesus' prayer in chapter 17 explicitly excludes those who do not believe, and the implication throughout is that they will face a judgment based on their own actions and attitudes.

Opposition

Throughout the Gospel there has been an escalating opposition to Jesus. This was anticipated in the Prologue, where the evangelist portrays Jesus as one who comes into the world that he created, but his own people reject him (1:10–11). This opposition is often termed "the world" and is portrayed as darkness.

In the final discourses, Jesus predicts that this opposition will extend to his followers as well. We have already seen that "the Jews" were attempting to kill Lazarus as well as Jesus (12:9–11), so this theme has already been introduced in the narrative leading up to the final discourses. But the Fourth Gospel discloses in a number of instances that the followers of Jesus in the future will face the opposition of "the world."

This theme is developed in three sections in the final discourses: 15:18–25; 16:29–33; and 17:12–16. In the first of these units, Jesus says that "the world" will oppose his followers in the same way that it currently opposes him. This prediction suggests a fundamental opposition between the thinking of the world and that of God—it is the opposition of darkness to light. Those who hate the believers are really indicating that they hate God, for hatred of Jesus is hatred of God.

According to the Fourth Gospel, this fundamental opposition to the message of Jesus will be manifested by opposition to all believers. But the opposition should not be seen as any failure on God's or Jesus' part. It is, instead, a part of the very nature of Jesus' mission—to shine light on the darkness and so bring about the crisis of judgment, either to belief or to death. But Jesus makes clear that his mission is ultimately victorious. Neither the cross nor subsequent opposition to his followers should suggest any failure—Jesus has conquered the world in his mission (16:33). But this also implies a period of time between the death of Jesus and the future demonstration of his victory. Although the ruler of this world is coming to demonstrate his power, he has no power over Jesus and, by implication, over the believers (14:30). One demonstration of Jesus' victory is seen in the future home of Christians ("I go to prepare a place for you," 14:2). Another demonstration of Jesus' power will be activity of the Paraclete in the community of believers.

Want to Know More?

About the meaning of Paraclete? See William Barclay, *New Testament Words* (Louisville: Westminster John Knox Press, 1974), 215–22.

About the metaphor of the vine? See Carol A. Newsom and Sharon H. Ringe, eds., *Women's Bible Commentary*, expanded ed. (Louisville, Ky.: Westminster John Knox Press, 1998), 391–92.

The sense of impending opposition is reiterated in Jesus' final prayer, when he acknowledges that his disciples' belief in him means they are "not of this world." Thus, followers of Jesus, by their belief, become separate from the world and subject to opposition. So Jesus prays that they be protected from the evil one in this life. However, he specifically does not pray that they be somehow withdrawn from the world, only that they be protected in the midst of opposition (17:15). The life of the believer, then, is to be the same as Jesus' own life—active engagement with the world, with the aim that more will come to believe. The same opposition that faced Jesus is to face his followers, for they continue the very work of the master.

Jesus' Self-Disclosure in the Farewell Speeches

As indicated previously, John's Gospel is noteworthy for the way in which the narrative is punctuated at various points with long dialogues or discourses by Jesus, many of them self-revelatory in a way in which the Synoptic Gospels never portray Jesus. The extended discourse found in chapters 14–17 is certainly no exception to this pattern. In these final speeches, Jesus discloses more about his divine nature, his relationship with God, and his future relationship with the disciples than anywhere previously in the Gospel. In many places his speech echoes the "I am" format, but in other places Jesus discloses himself in significant ways without using the formula "I am." But the entire discourse is intensely theological and revelatory; in it, Jesus interprets his mission as the one sent from God who is returning to God, as the descending and ascending Word who alone is able to enlighten humanity.

In these final discourses, Jesus uses two explicit "I am" metaphors. In 14:6, he says that he is the way, the truth, and the life. Each of these attributes has already been introduced in the Gospel, but they are made more explicit here. In the Prologue, Jesus is said to be full of grace and truth (1:17), and the Gospel later says that he speaks the words of truth (e.g., 5:33; 8:45). Similarly, the Prologue opens with a reference to Jesus that "in him was life" (1:4). This reference to Jesus as giving life is reiterated a number of times: belief in him offers eternal life (e.g., 3:16, 36), and indeed, his purpose is to offer life to humanity (10:10). Moreover, the term *life* is used to modify a number of other self-referential attributes: he is the bread of life, the spring that brings forth life-giving waters, the light of life. The term *way* has been mentioned only once previously, in John's citation from Isaiah 40:3 (John 1:23). But the entire Gospel is the outworking of Jesus' way, his journey among people and his journey back to God. So Jesus' identification of himself as the way, the truth, and the life simply affirms what the reader already knows about Jesus from the Gospel narrative.

> **"I am . . ."**
>
> Some of the important "I am" discourses prior to the passion narrative are:
>
> Discourse with the Samaritan Woman—"I am he (the Christ)" (John 4)
>
> Discourse on the Bread—"I am the bread of life" (John 6)
>
> Discourses at Tabernacles—"I am the light of the world"; "Before Abraham was, I am" (John 8)
>
> Shepherd Discourse—"I am the door, I am the good shepherd" (John 10)
>
> Lazarus's Raising—"I am the resurrection and the life" (John 11)

As we have already discussed, chapter 15 introduces a new and substantial "I am" metaphor. Here, Jesus says that he is the true vine and that believers are the branches of the vine that bear fruit. The metaphor is important for developing his major theological theme of abiding, which we have already discussed. By the use of "I am" language this theme is strengthened, since all the "I am" metaphors share in the divine self-designation ("I am who I am") and provide crucial ways of understanding the importance of Jesus' ministry. There is, then, a cumulative force to these references that makes all the metaphors resonate with one another. The vine is thus added to the already long list of descriptions for Jesus: bread, light, good shepherd, way, truth, life.

But the self-revelatory features of the final discourse go beyond the clear "I am" metaphors. Throughout the entire discourse, Jesus is revealing openly his divine nature, his origination from God, and his unique relationship with God. In these revelatory statements, Jesus is affirming what the narrator told the reader in the Prologue—that Jesus is the unique Son of God, participating in the actual nature of God. Thus, when Jesus declares, "I am in the Father and the Father in me" (14:11), he is affirming that he shares a complete intimate existence with God (an echo of the Prologue's "the Word was with God, and the Word was God"). When he says, "I came from the Father and have come into the world" (16:28) and "I do not belong to the world" (17:14), one can again hear the echo of the Prologue's language: "He was in the world, and the world came into being through him; yet the world did not know him. He came to what was his own, and his own people did not accept him" (1:10–11). And Jesus' prayer to the effect that he desires his disciples "to see my glory, which you [God] have given me because you loved me before the foundation of the world" (17:24) reminds the reader again of the poetic language of the Prologue: "In the beginning was the Word, and the Word was with God. . . . And the Word became flesh and lived among us, and we have seen his glory, the glory as of a father's only son, full of grace and truth" (1:1, 14).

The final discourse, set just before Jesus' arrest and death, brings us back to the beginning point of the Gospel. It serves to remind us of who Jesus truly is: the Word of God incarnate. And in doing so, it is both the final (in terms of time but also of ultimacy) teaching and the framework for the ultimate irony—the death of the life giver, who by dying gives life.

? Questions for Reflection

1. What different roles does Jesus say the Paraclete will play? Reread John 14:15–17, 25–26; 15:26–27; 16:7–11, 12–15.
2. "I am the true vine," Jesus says in John 15:1. What does he mean? What is required of his followers for them to "bear fruit"?
3. What do you think the disciples understood of Jesus' departure? How, when, and where did they think they would see him again?
4. John writes extensively about the opposition to Jesus. Who/what would he see as Jesus' opposition today?

John 18–19

The Trial and Crucifixion of Jesus

The Fourth Gospel's account of the arrest and trial of Jesus is both similar to and different from the other Gospel accounts. In the broad details—that Jesus was arrested on the Mount of Olives, that he was taken to the Jewish high priest and subsequently delivered to Pilate, that Peter denied him at the high priest's house, and that Jesus was ultimately sentenced to death by hanging on a cross—John agrees with the Synoptics. But in a number of the ways in which the narrative is developed, we can see John's unique perspective, a perspective that probably retains significant historical details even while showing the Fourth Evangelist's theological understanding of the event.

It is important to remember that certain aspects of the Fourth Gospel's presentation of the events leading up to the arrest and trial create a framework that is different from the Synoptic Gospel accounts. For instance, in John "the Jews" have already met and formally "convicted" Jesus in their council (11:45–53). Indeed, the mounting opposition of "the Jews" toward Jesus has been a major theme throughout the entire Gospel. And we have already seen that Jesus' final meal was on the day before the Passover, not on the Passover itself. In addition to these narrative features, the Fourth Evangelist has already painted a picture of Jesus' speech in which he has been explicit about Jesus' mission and his nature. Jesus has demonstrated to a significant degree his knowledge of God's plan and his own intentional purpose with respect to fulfilling that plan, especially in the final discourses (chapters 14–17). All these features of the Fourth Gospel have a bearing on how the arrest, trial, and crucifixion account is told.

The Arrest of Jesus (18:1–14)

After the final discourses of Jesus, the scene shifts from the room where the dinner has taken place to the Mount of Olives. In the Fourth Evangelist's description, this is a garden across the valley of Kidron. It is important for the evangelist to note that Judas knew this place because the disciples had often met there, for in John's account Judas left the disciples at the close of the Last Supper. The knowledge of where Jesus frequently went allows Judas to lead the arresting party to him.

John's account has no record of a final prayer, especially no "agonizing" prayer such as that found in Mark. We have noted already, however, that John reports two prayers in the passion week, which perhaps capture some of this sense of a final conversation with God. The first was just before the Passover week, in 12:27–28, when Jesus indicated that his heart was troubled yet refused to ask for God to rescue him from the coming events. This occasion saw a response from God in the form of a voice from heaven. The second is the long priestly prayer in John 17, in which Jesus prays for his disciples and those who will believe in subsequent generations. So the essence of Jesus conversing with God in prayer in the final week is found in the Fourth Gospel, but not in the form found in the Synoptics, and the sense that Jesus is in anguish over the impending events is not present. Indeed, throughout the Gospel, Jesus is portrayed as intentional, knowledgeable, and fairly self-confident in the face of the growing opposition and his death.

Judas arrives at the garden on the Mount of Olives with a contingent of soldiers and officers from the high priests

Key Players

Peter: Also known as Simon Peter, he was a Galilean and one of the twelve disciples of Jesus. His name means "rock." Known for his impetuousness, Peter cut off the ear of the high priest's slave when the soldiers tried to arrest Jesus. He then denied knowing Jesus three times, as Jesus predicted he would, but went on to become one of the great leaders of the early church. He was eventually crucified—tradition has it, upside down, because he said he was not worthy to be crucified in the same way as Christ.

Pilate: Pontius Pilate was Roman governor of Judea from 26 to 36 C.E. The Jewish authorities brought Jesus before him for punishment. Somewhat reluctant, Pilate instead asked the gathered crowd if they wanted him to release Jesus. (It may have been a Jewish custom or a custom of Pilate to release a prisoner at Passover.) But instead they called for him to release Barabbas, and Pilate eventually "washed his hands" of the affair and handed Jesus over to be crucified. Tradition has it that he was later removed from office by the Roman authorities for ordering a massacre of innocent Galileans (see Luke 13:1) and returned to Rome and committed suicide.

Barabbas: Barabbas was a bandit or, perhaps, a rebel against Roman rule. Mark and Luke also say that Barabbas was a murderer.

105

and the Pharisees. The first group, the soldiers, seems to suggest Roman involvement in the arrest, which has raised eyebrows among commentators. But that the evangelist understood this to be case is confirmed in 18:12, where a distinction is made between the soldiers and "Jewish police." Is it possible that the Roman government would have cooperated at this level with the Jewish leadership? Or is this instead a way for John to indicate that the whole world participated in the rejection of Jesus? The latter, theological concept seems strained; as we shall see, John understands the Romans to be only passively involved in the death of Jesus. The second group mentioned at the arrest, the officers from the chief priests and Pharisees, connects the arresting party directly to the group who condemned Jesus. In John, when "the Jews" try to arrest Jesus, it is at the instigation of the "chief priests and Pharisees." This arrest scene is thus linked to both 7:32–36 and 11:47–53.

When the arresting party arrives, there is no kiss of identification, nor any need for it. Jesus instead takes the initiative by asking whom they seek, and in response to their request for "Jesus of Nazareth," he openly identifies himself to the arresting party. This particular scene has a curious element to it. On hearing him identify himself—"I am he"—the arresting party step back and fall to the ground. Why? Is it possible that the Jewish guards prostrated themselves on hearing him use the phrase "I am he"—literally, the "I am" (*ego eimi*) he used in his self-revelatory metaphors, which echoes the divine self-designation in Exodus 3:14? This seems unlikely given the guards' knowledge of his teaching and their orders to arrest him. More likely, this "falling down" is meant to illustrate symbolically that they "stumbled" at this point over the very one who came as their savior.

The Fourth Gospel contains a detailed portrayal of the arresting officer's ear being cut off. The evangelist indicates that it was Peter who struck the blow, and this impetuous action coheres with what we know about Peter, from both the Fourth Gospel and the other Gospels. The scene concludes with Jesus stopping the resistance; he will not support any opposition to the arrest, for it is the necessary prelude to the "cup" God has set before him to drink.

The arresting officials then take Jesus to the house of the high priest. But curiously, the Fourth Evangelist reports that Jesus was taken first to Annas, the father-in-law of the current high priest, Caiaphas. Only secondarily is Jesus taken to Caiaphas (18:24), and nothing of the latter exchange is recorded. The hearing before Annas (18:19–24) once again affirms Jesus' openness and self-confidence in the face of persecution. The scene draws heavily on language related to forensic rhetoric of the type that has been used throughout the Gospel: testimony, signs, truth, judgment, and proof (or belief). Throughout the Gospel, Jesus has defended himself openly against unjust persecution, and once again he is put in the position of the accused. Jesus indicates, as the narrative of the Fourth Gospel has related, that he has taught openly in the Temple and synagogues. As a result, everyone has had the opportunity to hear his message and to assess his character. In other words, Jesus has functioned as a faithful witness, being open before all. In contrast, it would seem, this hearing before the high priest, held at night and not open to all, violates the sense of justice. And in response to Jesus' simple statement affirming his openness, he is struck by the high priest's officer—a senseless act of brutality. At stake here are basic concepts of justice: true testimony and a fair trial. Jesus is both the true witness and the innocent victim of unjust persecution.

> **Annas and Caiaphas**
>
> It seems fairly clear that Annas was the high priest during Jesus' youth, between 6 C.E. and 15 C.E. Annas is also linked to Caiaphas by Luke in two separate accounts. In Luke 3:2, the beginning of John the Baptist's ministry was said to be in the priesthood of Annas and Caiaphas. This may refer to Annas as the most recent high priest (deposed by Valerius Gratus) and Caiaphas as the current high priest. Similarly, Luke records in Acts 4:6 that Peter was brought before Annas the high priest, together with Caiaphas and John and Alexander and the rest of the high-priestly family. In this designation, Luke seems to record a memory of how the high-priestly family functioned very similar to John's.

Peter's Denial (18:15–27)

As in all the Gospels, Peter denies his Lord three times while Jesus is being questioned by the high priest. In all the Gospels, this denial is predicted at the Last Supper. In this respect John is remarkably similar to the Synoptics, even while the details differ.

In John's account, Peter is accompanied by another disciple. This other, unnamed disciple is known by the high priest; this explains how he and Peter were able to gain access to the courtyard of the high priest, a feature left unexplained in the other Gospels. During the course of the night, while joining the various officers and servants of the high priests around warming fires, Peter is questioned about his relationship to Jesus, who himself is being questioned inside. Peter denies being a disciple of Jesus and denies being present at the arrest.

Despite the fact that Peter denies Jesus, there is still a fairly positive interpretation of Peter in this account. Peter never denies knowing Jesus, only being one of his disciples. And the third denial, by being linked to the incident in the garden, may be seen as an attempt to escape arrest or retribution for the assault. In contrast, Mark portrays Peter swearing an oath that he never knew Jesus, a much more emphatic and negative portrayal of Peter. Here, rather than an outright denial of Jesus himself, we simply see a weak Peter who is still open to redemption—which is indeed the rest of the story in John.

> "The essence of the matter was that it was the real Peter who protested his loyalty in the upper room; it was the real Peter who drew his lonely sword in the moonlight of the garden; it was the real Peter who followed Jesus, because he could not allow his Lord to go alone; it was *not* the real Peter who cracked beneath the tension and denied his Lord. *And that is just what Jesus could see.*"—Barclay, *Gospel of John*, vol. 2, 231.

Pilate's Trial (18:28–19:16)

John's version of the trial before Pilate is striking in its construction, the portrayal of Pilate, and the impression one gets of the Jewish opposition to Jesus. All these elements combine to make this trial scene compelling and interesting, as well as a theological statement of the conflict between Jesus and leaders of the Jewish people.

The trial begins with Jesus being taken to Pilate's headquarters, the praetorium. In an uncharacteristic note of vagueness, John simply reports that "they" brought Jesus to Pilate, without any clarity about who "they" are. One might imagine they are the chief priests and Pharisees, who ordered the arrest, together with the Temple police. But later on we learn that it is "the Jews" who respond to Pilate's questions. Perhaps this means the term *the Jews* should be equated with the leadership of the Jewish council. But previously in the Gospel, "the Jews" had a broader meaning than that narrow definition. Pilate himself refers to the group who accuse Jesus as being "your own nation and the chief priests" (18:35), which seems to imply broad participation in the accusing party. Instead of a small group of Jewish leaders, it seems that at the point of taking Jesus to trial, those accompanying Jesus are a broader group. Certainly, this term is meant to symbolize all those who should know that Jesus is the Messiah (his people) but who reject him nonetheless.

In the opening of the trial before Pilate, the Fourth Evangelist reminds the reader of his unique chronology of the Passover week: it is not yet Passover, and so the deputation from the chief priest is unwilling to enter the praetorium lest they become ritually unclean and thus unable to enter the Temple for the sacrifice of the Passover lambs. This group of opponents is thus closely linked to the Jewish religious life, which only increases the irony of their prosecution of the Son of God. As a result of the Fourth Gospel's chronology, the events that follow take place in two different settings: the interrogation by Pilate takes place inside the praetorium, whereas Pilate's interaction with the Jewish leaders and the crowds takes place outside. Thus, Pilate is seen as shuttling back and forth between Jesus and the crowd. This split between the settings allows Pilate to have private, almost intimate conversations with Jesus, which is a hallmark of the Fourth Gospel's trial setting and at the same time adds a certain narrative action to a relatively long unit of text. At any rate, the contrast between Jesus and his opponents is heightened by the physical separation, and almost by necessity, Pilate is put in the position of mediator between the two.

The trial begins with the formal accusation, which Pilate demands at the outset. The response by "the Jews" is certainly weak and non-specific: "If this man were not a criminal, we would not have handed him over to you" (18:30). But we also learn that they want the death penalty for Jesus; it is only for this reason that they hand him over to Pilate. It is perhaps implied that one of the charges is that Jesus claims to be "King of the Jews," since the first question Pilate asks him is whether he is King of the Jews. But in response to Jesus' question whether that is one of the charges against him ("Do you ask this on your own, or did others tell you about me?"—18:34), Pilate says only that the Jews have handed him over, not that they accused him of this. The net effect is of rather vague charges that do not point to any specific violation of law.

In the trial, Pilate is seen as pursuing a fairly gentle interrogation. He asks a number of times if Jesus is King of the Jews, to which Jesus gives deflective answers: "My kingdom is not from this world" (18:36); "You say that I am a

> "The Evangelist conducts no polemic against the power of the Empire such as is found in Revelation. He does not provide the raw material for anything like a church-state confrontation. What he presents is a pagan protagonist of unbelief to balance off his Judean ones who, because of their background, should have believed."—Sloyan, *John*, Interpretation, 206.

king" (18:37). Such indirect answers do not seem to perturb Pilate, and in response to Jesus' primary claim, that he came into the world to testify to the truth, Pilate responds more with curiosity than with accusation: "What is truth?" (18:38). Even in 19:11, when Jesus says that Pilate could have power over him only if he (Jesus) willed it, Pilate does not get angry but instead seeks to release Jesus. Still, Pilate is not painted with completely rosy colors. He has Jesus flogged and humiliated, apparently a normal course of events for an accused criminal (19:1–5). But despite this, the overall portrayal of Pilate is not negative.

Pilate's judgment throughout this trial is that Jesus should be released. He repeats this three times. In the first instance, after his initial interrogation, he attempts to use the Passover practice of releasing a convicted criminal as a means of releasing Jesus. But "the Jews" demand Barabbas, an insurrectionist, be released instead. After having Jesus flogged and dressing him up as a king for public humiliation, Pilate again seeks to have him released. And finally, after a third interrogation, Pilate resolves again to release him. Only when "the Jews" suggest that to release Jesus would mean that Pilate was opposing the emperor does Pilate hand Jesus over to crucifixion.

"The Jews," by contrast, are portrayed with an increasing animus toward Jesus that leads them, ironically, to convict themselves, at least before God. They not only bring Jesus to Pilate for conviction but press the death penalty as the appropriate punishment for vague and unsubstantiated charges. When Pilate offers Jesus as a possible Passover release, they choose a convicted criminal instead. When Pilate brings out Jesus, dressed in purple, and announces, "Here is the man!" they cry out emphatically, "Crucify him! Crucify him!" (19:6). And when Pilate still seeks to release Jesus, they use political blackmail against Pilate, suggesting that to release Jesus would be regarded as treason against Caesar. The emotion of "the Jews'" reaction reaches a fever pitch in the last scene. Faced one more time with Jesus on the judge's bench outside the praetorium, with Pilate proclaiming, "Here is your king!" they respond emphatically: "Away with him! Away with him! Crucify him!" (19:15).

The ultimate irony in the presentation of "the Jews'" opposition is found in the final response to Pilate's question of whether they truly want Jesus crucified. When he asks, "Shall I crucify your King?" (19:15), they respond by saying, "We have no king but the emperor." It is clear that they cannot accept Jesus as king, but in their emphatic rejection of Jesus, they betray their God as well. To affirm no king but the emperor is to deny God as king. This is a fulfillment of what Jesus accused them earlier in the Gospel. When faced with their rejection of him, Jesus declared that God was not in fact their Father because they rejected God; rather, they were children of the devil, who was a murderer and a liar (8:42–44).

The trial ends with Pilate agreeing to the crucifixion (19:16). The text is not clear on whether the Romans or "the Jews" will crucify Jesus. On the one hand, "the Jews" earlier stated that they were not permitted by law to put anyone to death (18:31); and Pilate himself asked, "Shall I crucify your King?" (19:15). On the other hand, the narrative flow seems to suggest that "the Jews" actually carry out crucifixion. Pilate hands Jesus "over to them to be crucified." And as the scene shifts, John tells us that "they" took Jesus. The only reference to "them" in the previous two chapters has been to the Jewish opponents of Jesus. As Pilate finally relents to the pressure of the crowd, it appears that he simply turns over Jesus to them for crucifixion, rather than actively subjecting Jesus to Roman punishment.

"The Jews"

Given the intensity of the opposition to Jesus in the final chapters of John, it is worthwhile to revisit the question of who "the Jews" are and how we should interpret this story. As we discussed in Unit 2, it does not do justice to the overall presentation of the Fourth Gospel to equate "the Jews" with inhabitants of Judea; this is not simply a geographical reference. Nor is it to be taken as a criticism of Judaism as a religion. John presents a Jesus who actively goes to the Temple during the various festivals, who affirms the priority of Judaism over the Samaritan understanding of God, who cites Abraham and Moses as authoritative figures. And the vast majority of followers of Jesus are clearly Jewish, including some from the ranks of the leaders. So it is not Judaism that is to be seen as the opponent of Jesus. It would be more appropriate to cite the religious leaders, especially the chief priests and Pharisees in the final chapters, as being at the core of the group "the Jews" in John's Gospel. But even this identification is not exact; at a number of places in the Gospel, a distinction is made between "the Jews" and the leaders.

The term *the Jews* seems instead to be a literary fiction, a composite group, drawn out of Judaism to be sure, who oppose Jesus' ministry and his witness. In using this term, John has in essence created a character in the Gospel, one with an identifiable trait—consistent opposition to Jesus—which allows the conflict with Jesus to be easily portrayed. But throughout the Gospel, John has also made it clear that this is not easily translatable into a unified historical group. Not all leaders oppose Jesus. (Nicodemus, for instance, is at least open to him.) Not all the Jewish people oppose him. At times, some of the Jews believe, others do not. So the story of the Jewish people's reaction to Jesus is similar to our own—some believe, others do not. Yet, at the same time, John can summarize the opposition by using the shorthand term *the Jews.*

It is, therefore, important to understand the difference between the historical people of Israel, the Jews, and John's narrow use of "the Jews" and not to read too much into "the Jews," especially since John places the greatest guilt for Jesus' death on their shoulders. This should not occasion a broad charge that all Jews, or Judaism itself, share the guilt of Jesus' death. Indeed, the Gospel is presented from the standpoint of Judaism, and belief takes place within all levels of Judaism; "salvation is from the Jews" (4:22). By recognizing the term as a literary one by which the evangelist is able to emphasize the idea that Jesus was rejected even by those who should have known him and accepted him, we can read the Gospel for its fundamental message about the God who overcomes opposition and darkness, which exists even among those who claim God.

The Crucifixion (19:17–37)

Unlike the procession to Golgotha in other Gospels, Jesus in the Fourth Gospel carries the cross himself. He is crucified with two others, as all the Gospels report, but John has little interest in those who are being crucified with him. Instead, John directs our attention once more to the battle over Jesus' title. Pilate insisted that he have the title "King of the Jews" posted on the cross in three languages: Hebrew, Latin, and Greek. When "the Jews" object to the title, Pilate insists on it—a final snub to the Jewish opponents and, ultimately, a prophetic statement from Pilate.

John has not generally made extensive use of Old Testament passages as proof texts in support of the events of Jesus' life. But beginning with the passion narrative, the evangelist pays more attention to the connection of events to the Old Testament scriptures. Leading up to the Passover, the Fourth Evangelist cited Zechariah 9:9 to explain the donkey that Jesus rode when he entered Jerusalem for the last time and used Isaiah 53:1 and 6:10 to explain the rejection of Jesus by "the Jews." The crucifixion scene, however, finds a number of references to the Old Testament, specifically to indicate a fulfillment of scripture. In 19:24, Psalm 22:18 is used as proof text for the fact that Jesus' tunic is not torn into pieces but is distributed to the soldiers by lots. The reference to soldiers casting lots for Jesus' clothes is found in all the Gospels, but none except John's Gospel refers to a proof text for the episode. Similarly, the Fourth Gospel reports that the Jewish authorities asked that Jesus' legs be broken so that he should die before the Sabbath/Passover festival. But when Jesus is found dead already and thus does not need his legs

> "What does John mean to convey by the lance-thrust into Jesus' side that immediately drew blood and water? . . . This much, at least, is meant: that the mixed stream which came forth from Jesus in death achieved life for believing humanity."—Sloyan, *John*, Interpretation, 213.

broken, this is said to be the fulfillment of Exodus 12:46, which commands that the bones of the Passover lamb not be broken. And finally, on finding Jesus dead, the soldiers pierce his side and it issues forth blood and water. This piercing is said to be the fulfillment of Zechariah 12:10, which describes how they will look upon the one whom they have pierced. The order to break Jesus' legs and the piercing of his side are unique to John; and the latter, at least, is significant, since his pierced side will be important in the postresurrection appearances (20:20, 25, 27).

The crucifixion

A poignant scene is related while Jesus hangs on the cross. Jesus' mother and the beloved disciple are present at the crucifixion, along with some other women. Jesus addresses his mother, just like at Cana, as "woman" and, referring to the beloved disciple, says, "Here is your son." Similarly, he addresses the beloved disciple and says, "Here is your mother." Given that the disciple then takes Jesus' mother into his house, this must signify some kind of adoption whereby the beloved disciple is assigned special care of Jesus' mother. But given the previous appearance of his mother at Cana and the similarities between these two accounts, the reader is undoubtedly expected to draw some conclusions about these two events. In both, the only scenes in the Gospel in which Jesus' mother appears, he calls her "woman." At Cana, Jesus says his hour is not yet come. Clearly, on the cross his hour is come. The miracle at Cana exposed his glory to his disciples; the death and resurrection are his glorification. These similarities suggest that the beloved disciple's "adoption" is meant somehow to signify the completion, the fulfillment, of Jesus' ministry. With his mother now cared for by the beloved disciple, with the future of his family and his disciples linked, he has completed his task. It is, then, significant that Jesus goes on shortly to say, "It is finished."

Jesus' death in the Fourth Gospel lacks any cry of dereliction from the cross such as Mark and Matthew report. Instead he cries, "It is finished," and gives up his spirit. He remains in control of events, as he indicated to Pilate he would. With Jesus remains the power over his crucifixion and his death. Dying is his intentional act. For the Fourth Gospel, Jesus is the knowing Son, the preexistent Word, who now returns to the Father. As the Gospel has affirmed throughout, in this "lifting up," Jesus is glorified.

Jesus' Burial (19:38–42)

The opposition of "the Jews" is seen even in the burial. Joseph of Arimathea asks for and receives the body of Jesus. Joseph, the Gospel tells us, is a disciple of Jesus, but a secret one because of fear of "the Jews." Here we are reminded of the parents of the blind man in chapter 9, who fear being removed from the synagogue by "the Jews," as well as of authorities cited in 12:42 who fear to declare their faith openly, lest they also be removed from the synagogue.

Joseph is joined by Nicodemus, who has been an ambiguous character in the Gospel. Is Nicodemus a disciple too? In the previous scenes where Nicodemus appeared (3:1–15; 7:50), it was not clear whether he truly believed in Jesus or was only open to the possibility that Jesus was the Messiah. Here, at the burial scene, Nicodemus remains an ambiguous figure. While Joseph is called a secret disciple, Nicodemus is not. Does he perhaps illustrate the righteous Jew who seeks to fulfill proper burial customs yet who is not yet willing to believe in Jesus? Or does his inclusion in the story suggest that he has, in fact, come to believe?

Joseph and Nicodemus attend to the task of burying Jesus according to the Jewish practices, with spices and burial cloths. It should be noted that this act of burial, although an important part of Jewish culture, made them "impure" and hence unable to go to the Temple for a period of time. It was therefore a sacrifice on their part, which certainly denotes their respect for Jesus. The Fourth Gospel indicates that Jesus was laid in a tomb that had never been used, although the reason for its use was that it was close at hand—which is important because the Sabbath was coming upon them. The new tomb does not itself indicate any particular sign of respect or purity. Jewish burial practice was to place the deceased in a tomb, generally a family tomb, for a period of decomposition, then a year later to collect the bones and place them in a container. An unused tomb could, perhaps, be a sign of shame, an indication that no one was willing to offer a family tomb. But for John, the choice of tomb is a matter more of expediency than of anything else.

And thus the trial and crucifixion end on a note of sadness, despite the language of glorification. As darkness draws close, Jesus is hurriedly buried in a tomb apart from others. The burial is done in an atmosphere of "fear of the Jews." And his disciples are not present—perhaps also because of fear. Fear and darkness, and perhaps shame, have taken center stage as the curtain of Jesus' life is drawn shut.

Want to Know More?

About Pontius Pilate? See Mark Littleton, *Jesus: Everything You Need to Know to Figure Him Out* (Louisville, Ky.: Westminster John Knox Press, 2000), 123; Paul J. Achtemeier, ed., *HarperCollins Bible Dictionary*, rev. ed. (New York: HarperCollins, 1996), 855–56.

About Peter? See Paul J. Achtemeier, ed., *HarperCollins Bible Dictionary*, rev. ed. (New York: HarperCollins, 1996), 833–36.

? Questions for Reflection

1. In quick succession, Peter has the unenviable position of being first the rock of the church and then the agent of Satan. Perhaps there is only a fine line between the two. What helps make the distinction between the two?

2. The author of this study writes that "the overall portrayal of Pilate [in John] is not negative." Do you agree or disagree? What was Pilate hoping to accomplish?

3. Why did Pilate insist that the title "King of the Jews" be posted on Jesus' cross?

4. Have someone in your group read aloud each of the Gospel accounts of the crucifixion—Matthew 27:32–56; Mark 15:21–41; Luke 23:32–49; John 19:16–37. Discuss the differences and similarities between the different accounts. Look specifically at Jesus' last recorded words from the cross (Matt. 27:46; Mark 15:34; Luke 23:46; John 19:30). Which of these Gospel accounts is easiest for you to accept? Why?

10 John 20–21

The Resurrection Appearances of Jesus

The Fourth Gospel relates the crucifixion and death of Jesus as a victory, one in which Jesus willingly dies in order to fulfill his mission and thus to glorify God. In many ways, then, the death of Jesus brings to completion his role of revealing God in his actions, words, and finally his death. But the story is not finished. As Jesus indicated in his farewell discourses, there is a future to the story that involves his followers. They are to receive the Spirit; they are to continue to testify; there are to be future followers who come to believe based on the testimony of the disciples. With chapters 20 and 21, John turns to the beginning of this "rest of the story."

Numerous times the narrator has informed us that the disciples, while they believed in Jesus, came to know the full import of his actions only after he was glorified. For instance, the Temple incident in chapter 2 suggested that at the time the disciples did not completely understand but that after Jesus' death they would come to understand and contextualize his sayings about "this temple," which was his body (2:22). Similarly, at the triumphal entry, the disciples are said to have lacked understanding of the importance of the entrance on a donkey, but they would come to understand after his death (12:16). An anticipation of the coming of the Spirit, the Paraclete, has also been repeated (7:37–39; 14:26; 15:26; 16:13), and this Paraclete is to bring understanding and remembrance. We have been led to expect, then, the arrival of full understanding after Jesus' death. The events following Jesus' death, in which the disciples confront the full meaning of his life and death, have been anticipated in the narrative of Jesus' life.

The Empty Tomb (20:1–10)

As in all the Gospels, the first to arrive at the empty tomb on Sunday morning is Mary Magdalene. In John's Gospel she comes alone, not with other women. Mary's initial reaction seems to be influenced by the preceding opposition to Jesus. She concludes that, since the stone has been rolled away and Jesus' body is missing, "they" have removed it. One can conclude that the "they" she speaks about are the Jewish opposition to Jesus. There is no hint of belief that Jesus might be raised from the dead. Indeed, the very setting of Mary's arrival at the tomb—while it is still dark—implies her unbelief, for John has used this darkness motif frequently to describe those who either do not understand or disbelieve (cf. Nicodemus's meeting in 3:1, as well as the betrayal by Judas). But Mary returns immediately to the disciples and includes them in her ignorance of what has happened by using the inclusive "we": "we do not know where they have laid him" (20:2).

Two key disciples, then, rush to the tomb to confirm Mary's report. The beloved disciple—who has become a key, if mysterious, figure in the passion narrative (13:23; 19:26)—and Simon Peter run to the tomb. The picture is one of a footrace in which the beloved disciple outruns Peter, perhaps as a sign of his personal anxiety over the missing body. And although the beloved disciple reaches the tomb first and, peering in, confirms the absence of Jesus' body and the presence of the linen cloths, it is Peter who first enters the tomb. The picture is of an empty tomb, with grave cloths in two piles, one of which is the face covering, folded apart from the other clothes. Clearly something significant has happened, and it is not just the removal of the body to another tomb.

> "The fact that it is women who are portrayed as the first witnesses of Jesus' resurrection underlines the historical truth of the story, for no one in that culture would have invented a story that gave such a key role to women." —Donald A. Hagner, in *Life in the Face of Death: The Resurrection Message in the New Testament,* ed. Richard Longnecker (Grand Rapids: Wm. B. Eerdmans Publishing Co., 1998), 109.

The Fourth Evangelist's report of the empty tomb and especially the grave cloths is interesting, especially if we contrast this with the other resurrection in this Gospel. We might recall that when Lazarus was raised, John was very explicit in detailing how he came forth from the tomb with the grave cloths still wound around him and his face cloth still covering the face (11:44). In contrast to this "normal" situation,

Jesus' grave cloths are lying on the floor, with the face cloth off to one side. This is clearly not normal—something unusual has occurred, and it is not simply the resurrection of a dead man. The unusual placement of the cloths is meant to signify something, and that is the activity of God.

Of the two disciples to see the empty tomb, the beloved disciple is given priority for, on seeing the empty tomb and the grave cloths lying in piles, he is said to believe. But in what does he believe? The disciples have already come to believe that Jesus is the Messiah, the one sent from God. Given the note of commentary that they did not yet know the scripture that Jesus must rise from the dead, the conclusion must be that the beloved disciple came to believe that Jesus was raised from the dead. The empty tomb, then, functions much as other signs in the Gospel have—it results in belief on the part of at least some who are present.

It is interesting to note, given the narrator's comment that the disciples did not yet know the scripture that Jesus must rise from the dead, that John's Gospel has never related Jesus predicting that he will rise from the dead. Unlike the Synoptic Gospels, which have Jesus predicting in his lifetime that he will die and after three days rise again (cf. Mark 8:31; 9:9, 31; 10:34; and parallels), John never has Jesus saying this, not even in the final discourses. Jesus promises the Spirit after his departure, he promises to bring the disciples to the place where he is going, but he never explicitly predicts that he will be raised from the dead. The disciples' and Mary's confusion, then, is understandable, and the beloved disciple's belief is all the more remarkable.

"Finally, the Resurrection did not just teach the disciples about Jesus, or about the future. It also taught them about God. It was the supreme moment of his revelation. In particular the Resurrection could be seen as the great moment when God had demonstrated his power and overcome evil. It was his moment of victory."—Peter Walker, *The Weekend That Changed the World* (Louisville, Ky.: Westminster John Knox Press, 2000), 187.

Mary in the Garden (20:11–18)

In contrast to the beloved disciple stands Mary. She is portrayed as having returned to the garden where the tomb is, and her weeping indicates a lack of understanding or belief in the resurrection. The two angels who appear in the tomb appropriately ask her, "Why are you weeping?" This exchange is similar to the angels' question in Luke, when they ask the women, "Why do you look for the living among the dead?" (Luke 24:5). But in the

Fourth Gospel, the risen Jesus himself then appears in the garden. Mary does not recognize him and mistakes him for a gardener. Only when he calls her by name does she recognize him as Jesus. It is curious that, having seen and heard the angels in the tomb, she would still ask Jesus, thinking him to be a gardener, where the body has been moved. This question underscores her lack of comprehension and belief.

The failure to recognize the risen Jesus is a familiar feature in other resurrection narratives. In Luke, the disciples going to Emmaus do not recognize Jesus until he breaks bread with them, nor do the disciples in the upper room. In both Luke and John, the risen Jesus is apparently not the same "person" as before—there has been a transformation, a change in form and substance—even though the risen Jesus is clearly physical in both. In John's account, the failure to recognize Jesus also underscores Mary's lack of any expectation of a risen Jesus and perhaps indicates her own lack of faith even after seeing and hearing angels in the tomb.

Upon recognizing Jesus, however, she responds with sincere emotion and touches him. But Mary's embrace serves only to emphasize the extreme disjunction between the earthly Jesus and the risen Jesus. This Jesus has not come back to live among them but is "on the way" to the Father; he is still to ascend, which is what he indicated in his farewell discourse—that he was going away. Still, one wonders why Jesus commands Mary not to touch him. Would her touch somehow confuse the physical and spiritual elements? While many translations suggest that she was attempting to "hold onto" him, as if she were trying to keep him there, the Greek only says, "Do not touch me," or, perhaps better, "Stop touching me." Yet later on Jesus invites Thomas to touch his hands and side. Does this mean that Jesus has ascended between his appearance to Mary and the subsequent appearance to Thomas? Or is there some other reason that Mary should not touch him? The difference of a week's time between these two appearances seems important, although no explanation is ever given for why this time should make a difference. But the command to Mary, which presumes that she has already touched him, at the very least affirms Jesus' physical presence in the garden.

With this appearance in the garden, however, Mary becomes the first to see the risen Lord. She returns to the disciples to announce the appearance and to set the stage for the subsequent appearances. Mary is given pride of place among those who see Jesus in his risen state and thus joins the beloved disciple in believing in the resurrection.

The Closed Room Appearances (20:19–29)

Later that day, the scene shifts to a gathering of the disciples in a locked room. The theme of the opposition of "the Jews" is continued, since the disciples are meeting behind a locked door for fear of "the Jews." Jesus appears in their midst, clearly a miraculous appearance. His initial words are "Peace be with you." This is reminiscent of the promise he gave them in his final discourse that he would give them peace (14:27). This distinctive greeting is repeated a number of times in the final appearances.

> "Some of my earliest church memories are of my family attending pancake suppers during the week in the basement of our church, where we would eat, sing the hymns of the faith, and discuss gospel or church matters. Too often today in the church the meal becomes an end in itself and not a means to Christian fellowship. We would do well to contemplate this text and see how this might be rectified."—Witherington, *John's Wisdom*, 359.

Jesus then shows the marks of his crucifixion—his hands and his side. The presentation of his hands and side is a very important feature in John's Gospel and pointedly affirms that the risen Jesus is truly a physical being, even when he is risen. It also reminds the reader that Jesus was truly a human being who suffered and died. In this emphasis on the hands and the side, reiterated in the appearance before Thomas, we find a continuity with the epistles of John. There, the author goes to great pains to emphasize the physical presence of Jesus. In the first epistle, John certifies that he truly saw Jesus and touched him with hands (1 John 1:1). Later on, John declares that only those with the Spirit of God confess that Jesus "has come in the flesh" (1 John 4:2). And in the second epistle also, John declares that deceivers are those who do not confess that "Jesus Christ has come in the flesh" (2 John 7). It appears that the evangelist is at great pains to refute a misconception about Jesus that he did not come in the flesh but only in the spirit. This misconception, called docetism, seems to have arisen at an early stage in the church's

> **Docetism**
>
> Docetism was the belief that Jesus only seemed or appeared to have a human body and to be a human person. This view was found during the period of the early church among Gnostics, who saw materiality as evil. It was condemned by Ignatius of Antioch (ca. 35–ca. 107). See Donald K. McKim, *Westminster Dictionary of Theological Terms* (Louisville, Ky.: Westminster John Knox Press, 1996), 81.

development. The Fourth Evangelist's multiple explicit comments about Jesus' appearance in the Gospel may well be an early effort to put this misconception to rest.

120

Jesus then proceeds to fulfill another of his promises from the final discourses, the giving of the Holy Spirit. He breathes on them commands that they should receive the Holy Spirit. The action of Jesus breathing on the disciples is suggestive, especially given the framework of the Prologue. Recall that the Prologue insisted Jesus was a coparticipant in the act of creation—"All things came into being through him, and without him not one thing came into being" (1:3)—and drew on the creation account from Genesis, "In the beginning . . ." (1:1; cf. Gen. 1:1). In John 20:22, Jesus' act echoes God's gift of life to humans in Genesis 2, "then the Lord God . . . breathed into his nostrils the breath of life; and the man became a living being" (Gen. 2:7). In the same way, Jesus breathes on the disciples and imparts the Holy Spirit, thus creating a new humanity and a new life.

With the gift of the Holy Spirit, the disciples are given a charge as his apostles (sent ones); they are sent to participate in the very mission Jesus had as a human. Notice that Jesus uses commissioning language: "As the Father has sent (*apostellō*) me, so I send (*apostellō*) you" (20:21). The giving of the Holy Spirit, then, confirms this commission and empowers them. Finally, they are charged to engage in the acts of forgiveness that have marked Jesus' ministry. This final charge is similar to a promise recorded in the Gospel of Matthew (18:18), where the promise of binding and releasing is given to the disciples. In Matthew as in John, the disciples are understood to continue Jesus' work after his departure.

This initial appearance to the disciples produces belief in the resurrection of Jesus. But Thomas was not present, and despite the witness of the other disciples, he remains unwilling to believe. A week later, then, Jesus appears again in a closed room, this time with Thomas present. As with the first appearance, this second appearance is on a Sunday, the first day of the week. Repeating the statement "Peace be with you," Jesus instructs Thomas to touch his feet and side, to certify that Jesus is indeed risen from the dead. The wounds in the hand and the side are understood to be the clear points of continuity with the crucified Jesus. Given the ability to actually touch the wounds of Christ, Thomas also declares his belief in Jesus.

The point of the sign, however, is to illustrate the variety of ways in which faith may arise. While Thomas is given the "sign," or evidence, of Jesus' resurrection by means of his actual touch, in much the same way that many in Jesus' time saw his various signs, this is not the only way faith can arise. Faith may also arise through the agency of the testimony, the true witness, which the disciples themselves will now offer. From this point on, belief will not come about by direct seeing but instead by the testimony of those who have seen. And belief in Jesus will arise in future hearers. Thomas's touch, then, is meant not primarily for him but rather to enable others, through his witness and the witness of the Fourth Gospel itself, to come to know Jesus and believe in him. It is a testimony for those who will follow in subsequent generations. "Blessed are those who have not seen and yet have come to believe" (20:29).

The Resurrection

The First Ending (20:30–31)

The final "sign" to Thomas has exemplified the purpose of the entire book, which the evangelist now makes clear in a concluding word. The signs recorded in this book are for the purpose of engendering belief in Jesus as the Christ, the Son of God. And this belief is life-giving. This is the purpose of the Gospel, this is the purpose of Jesus Christ: to give life to those who will see God's purpose and plan in the incarnation of the Word and act on it.

Each of the signs, then, is meant to serve the purpose of evidence or proof that will convince people about the reality of this person, Jesus. Belief (Greek, *pistis*) is the change of mind that comes about as a result of evidence and arguments about a proposition. Throughout the Gospel we have seen signs, testimony, and explanations by Jesus himself that have formed a complex argument: that God so loved the world that he sent the Word, God's Son, as a human to lead people to life-giving community through Jesus.

The Epilogue (Chapter 21)

The Fourth Gospel does not end, however, with the conclusion in 20:30–31. Instead, an entire chapter follows, with numerous appearances and more teaching. This story-after-the-story has led to vast amount of commentary. Many scholars believe that chapter 21 was added by a subsequent author or perhaps by the community to which the Fourth Gospel was originally written. Others believe that the Fourth Evangelist added the final chapter as an afterthought. Its placement after a seeming conclusion raises questions about the composition of the Gospel. And yet the final chapter retains much of the "feel" of the rest of the Gospel—stylistically, it is not remarkably different from the rest of the Gospel. While admittedly an extension of the Gospel, it is not clear that this chapter was written by anyone other than the Fourth Evangelist. There are

> "Chapter 21 poses squarely the problem of who are important before God in the work they do for the gospel. Congregations are much taken up with this problem. The clergy above all have it as a threat to their peace. The answer is a marvel of balance."—Sloyan, *John,* Interpretation, 232.

no major manuscripts that circulated without chapter 21. Instead, it seems to be an epilogue, an effort to address topics that are directly related not to belief in Jesus but rather to the ongoing life of the disciples.

It is probably not crucial whether the evangelist himself or someone very close to him wrote the epilogue. In the canon of scripture, the Fourth Gospel always contains the final chapter, and we are thus led to consider how it works in the Gospel and what important elements the final chapter adds for the reader.

The Fish Miracle (21:1–14)

The final chapter of John begins with another appearance by Jesus, this time in Galilee. A number of the disciples had gone to the Sea of Tiberias (this is John's normal reference for the Sea of Galilee) to fish. The disciples listed are Simon Peter, Thomas, Nathanael, the sons of Zebedee, and two others not named. Simon Peter is, of course, a major character in the Gospel, one of those called by Jesus in the first chapter and receiving special attention in the passion narrative. Thomas also received special attention in the resurrection appearance of chapter 20. Nathanael's interaction with Jesus is the subject of a major scene in the beginning of the Gospel (1:43–51). The only disciples listed in this postresurrection story who have not already been encountered in the Fourth Gospel are the sons of Zebedee. In the other Gospels these sons, James and John, are key characters. Despite their mention here, however, they are never named James and John, and they are almost insignificant parts of the story. Instead, just as in the final scenes of the passion narrative, Simon Peter and the disciple whom Jesus loved are the main characters.

These disciples are said to be fishing unsuccessfully when Jesus appears on the beach. The disciples do not recognize him but follow his direction to cast the net to the right side of the boat, whereupon they catch an exceedingly large number of fish. Seeing the miraculous catch, the disciple whom Jesus loved recognizes the person on the shore as Jesus and says so to Peter. Peter then dashes immediately to shore (after putting on some clothes). Thus Peter and the disciple whom Jesus loved are once again at center stage, and once again it is Peter who races to Jesus, just as he raced to the empty tomb.

On the shoreline, Jesus is roasting fish on a fire, with bread, yet he asks Peter to bring some of the fish (153 were caught) to him. They then all have breakfast, with Jesus distributing bread and fish to them. In this distribution of bread and fish, one is immediately reminded of the feeding of the five thousand (chapter 6), where Jesus distributes bread and fish to all.

The miraculous fish catch has some striking similarities to a fish catch related in Luke's Gospel. There (Luke 5:1–11) the cast of characters includes Simon Peter and the sons of Zebedee as well; Jesus instructs the disciples where to cast their nets after a disappointing night of fishing, and their nets fill with fish. In Luke, however, this serves as the basis for Peter, James, and John to follow Jesus; it is a call narrative, not a recognition story.

There are striking points of continuity and discontinuity between this story and the previous resurrection accounts. The narrator tells us this is the third time Jesus has appeared to the disciples since his resurrection, and indeed, this fits perfectly with the preceding accounts: first he appeared to the disciples in the closed room; then a week later to them, with Thomas present; and now at Galilee. And as at those appearances, he is definitely a physical being: in chapter 20, he showed his hands and side; here, he eats with the disciples. Moreover, as with the appearance to Mary in the garden, Jesus is not immediately recognizable—faith, born out of the miracle, leads the beloved disciple to understand that this must be Jesus. But why do the disciples not recognize Jesus after two previous appearances? And why do we now have the sons of Zebedee added, when they have been absent the entire Gospel?

The fish miracle at first glance seems somewhat out of place in the resurrection accounts. Previously, miracles or signs have been the occasion for Jesus to engage in a discourse or revelation about himself. But Jesus has now been fully revealed as the resurrected Son, so this is unnecessary. Instead, the miracle provides the setting for a dialogue between Simon Peter and Jesus that is oriented toward the future of the disciples, not toward imparting some information about Jesus himself. This appearance, then, shifts the focus away from Jesus' own life and resurrection to the lives of the believers and their community. In doing this, the epilogue fulfills a major emphasis of the final discourses (chapters 14–17) that also directed attention to the subsequent life of the followers of Jesus: the emphasis on the function of the Paraclete, the importance of love for one another, and the need for unity.

Jesus and Simon Peter (21:15–19)

The resulting dialogue between Jesus and Simon Peter both restores Peter to a central place after his denial and emphasizes his role in the developing community of believers. Jesus draws heavily on the imagery painted in chapter 10 of the good shepherd, applying it now to Peter.

Previously, Jesus personalized discipleship in terms of love—true disciples would love Jesus and would show that love by keeping his commandments (14:15, 21) or keeping his word (14:23). Jesus' question to Peter, "Do you love me?" (21:15), is thus consonant with the previous way of defining discipleship. When Peter responds affirmatively, Jesus gives him a specific command: "Feed my sheep." In doing this, Jesus transfers his own role of shepherd to Peter.

But Jesus does not simply ask this question and let it go. Instead, he asks Peter the question "Do you love me?"

> ### Peter's Martyrdom
>
> According to the Greek theologian Origen, Peter was crucified at Rome "with his head downward, as he himself had desired to suffer." He did this because he did not believe himself worthy to be crucified in the same manner as Jesus Christ.

three times (21:15, 16, 17). This triple repetition of the question, with Peter responding affirmatively each time, reminds one of Peter's triple denial of Jesus after Jesus' arrest. Although Peter failed there, he does not fail now. Despite having been denied, Jesus shows his love for Peter by giving him leadership, although that leadership will come at the price of suffering. But this, too, is the fulfillment of a previous word of Jesus. Peter, when faced with the prediction that he would deny Jesus, said he would follow Jesus even to the point of death. Jesus' response to Peter was that he could not follow him right then, "but you will follow afterward" (13:36). Peter would, like Jesus, be a shepherd, but he would also suffer and die in a way similar to the suffering and death of Jesus (21:18–19).

Much has been made of the variation in the language of Jesus' questions to Peter and Peter's responses. Two different words for "love" are used: *agapaō* and *phileō*. The first term is Jesus' usual term for love, used throughout the Gospel, and refers to a selfless love often associated with God's love toward people; the second term is a common term for brotherly love, but it also implies self-giving and consideration of the other first. In the first two questions, Jesus asks if Peter loves (*agapaō*) him, and Peter responds that yes, he loves (*phileō*) him. Jesus in the third question uses Peter's term (*phileō*), and Peter responds in kind. It has often been suggested that Peter's term in response to Jesus shows a tentative commitment, a lesser kind of love. But this is probably reading too much into the variations. Instead, the pattern shows a repeated declaration of love by Peter, and Jesus responds by entrusting him with the care of the flock, the believers in Jesus, in his absence.

A similar variation in language is used in Jesus' description of the believers and Peter's role with respect to them. The community of believers are variously called lambs (*arnia* the first time) and sheep (*probata* the other two times), although no clear distinction can be made between these two terms. This is the first time the former term is used in the Fourth Gospel, although the Revelation (whose authorship is also frequently ascribed to John) chooses it almost exclusively to refer to Jesus. And Jesus instructs Peter to feed the sheep and to shepherd them. Rather than seeking to understand the distinctions between the terms, it is probably more appropriate to see the overall pattern of threefold repetition and the emphatic quality of Jesus' exhortation and Peter's acceptance of it.

Simon Peter and the Beloved Disciple (21:20–23)

The theme of Peter's role in the new community of believers is developed in a new direction by comparison with the other key figure in the Fourth Gospel, "the disciple whom Jesus loved." Frequently, where Peter is a major character, there also the beloved disciple appears as a companion figure. Here, in the final scene of the Gospel, Peter is said to ask specifically about that disciple's role and his fate. It is not clear precisely what Peter's question with regard to the beloved disciple is. Is he asking what the beloved disciple's role in the community will be? Or is he asking about his fate? Jesus takes it as the latter, and the response simply defers an answer: "If it is my will that he remain until I come, what is that to you? Follow me!" (21:22). The response is clearly meant to reject comparisons, inviting instead total devotion to serving Christ.

The narrator informs us that this last word of Jesus was misinterpreted in the church, however. It was taken to mean that the beloved disciple would not die before Jesus came again. This suggests an expectation of Jesus' quick return, which was certainly a feature of the early church (cf. Mark 13:24–27; 1 Thess. 4:13–18). The comment in John 21:23 has often occasioned surprise, as if the Fourth Gospel had no concept of a second return of Jesus. But 5:27–29 and 14:3 can both be read as implying an eschatological return, not that different from Mark 13. Even here, the epilogue of John is not clearly distinct in theology or viewpoint from the rest of the Gospel.

Who Was "the Beloved Disciple"?

There are many theories about who the person referred to in John as "the beloved" really was. The traditional view was that it was John the son of Zebedee, brother of James. Other views held that it was Lazarus, Mary, John Mark (a companion of Peter), or another, unnamed disciple. However, neither scripture nor church tradition has conclusively identified "the beloved disciple."

The Second Ending (21:24–25)

With this discourse between Jesus and the disciples, the Gospel closes. This ending is meant to certify the truth of the Gospel itself. It returns to the theme of witness, which has been a feature throughout the Gospel. The validity of the author's witness and the truth of the message are vouchsafed because they are based on eyewitness. The author of the Gospel is identified with the beloved disciple—this is the natural way to understand the "this" introducing 21:24. Being based on the eyewitness of an actual disciple—the very disciple whom Jesus loved—the testimony of the Gospel is thus true and can be counted on. While not necessarily complete, it is yet accurate.

But who is the beloved disciple? Is it John, the brother of James known from the other Gospels? If so, then the appearance of the sons of Zebedee in the beginning of the epilogue may make some sense. Or is it another, unnamed disciple, one who was reluctant to list his or her name? A long list of possibilities in addition to John has been proposed, the most common being Lazarus (whom Jesus clearly loved), Mary (who was a follower of Jesus), and John Mark (who was closely linked with Peter, the constant companion of the beloved disciple). It must be said, however, that none of these can be positively identified by either the Gospel or church tradition. It is tempting to think of the beloved disciple as simply a literary construction, but that does not do justice to the ending, which ties the truth of the Gospel to the beloved disciple's participation in the events that have been told. In the end, the identity of the beloved disciple and of the author of the Fourth Gospel remains a puzzle.

Want to Know More?

About resurrection? See Shirley C. Guthrie, *Christian Doctrine*, rev. ed. (Louisville, Ky.: Westminster John Knox Press, 1994), 270–88.

? Questions for Reflection

1. "Do not hold on to me," Jesus said to Mary (20:17). What did Jesus mean by this? How, today, do we try to "hold onto" Jesus?
2. The resurrection can seem incredible, if not impossible, to our scientific minds. What are some images you can use to explain resurrection to someone who is not familiar with John's Gospel?
3. If your group has studied one or more of the Synoptic Gospels, compare and contrast them with John. What are some of the key differences in John? What is the "theme" of John?
4. At the end of this study of John's Gospel, how has your understanding of the life, ministry, death, and resurrection of Jesus been changed?

Bibliography

Barclay, William. *The Gospel of John.* New Daily Study Bible. 2 vols. Louisville, Ky.: Westminster John Knox Press, 2001.

———. *New Testament Words.* Louisville, Ky.: Westminster John Knox Press, 1974.

Brown, Raymond. *John.* Anchor Bible Series. 2 vols. Garden City, NJ: Doubleday, 1966, 1970.

Calvin, John. *The Institutes of the Christian Religion.* 2 vols. Edited by John T. McNeill, translated by Ford Lewis Battles. Philadelphia: Westminster Press, 1960.

Gench, Frances Taylor. *Women and the Word: Studies in the Gospel of John.* Louisville: Presbyterian Women, PC(USA), 2000.

Kysar, Robert. *John: The Maverick Gospel.* Louisville, Ky.: Westminster John Knox Press, 1993.

Newsom, Carol A., and Sharon H. Ringe, eds. *Women's Bible Commentary.* Expanded ed. Louisville, Ky.: Westminster John Knox Press, 1998.

Ramsay, William M. *The Westminster Guide to the Books of the Bible.* Louisville, Ky.: Westminster John Knox Press, 1994.

Rhodes, Arthur B. *The Mighty Acts of God.* Revised by W. Eugene March. Louisville, Ky.: Geneva Press, 2000.

Robinson, J. A. T. *The Priority of John.* Oak Park, IL: Meyer-Stone Books, 1987.

Sloyan, Gerard. *John.* Interpretation: A Commentary for Teaching and Preaching. Atlanta: John Knox Press, 1988.

Smith, D. Moody Jr. *John.* Nashville: Abingdon Press, 1999.

Witherington, Ben III. *John's Wisdom: A Commentary on the Fourth Gospel.* Louisville, Ky.: Westminster John Knox Press, 1995.

Interpretation Bible Studies
Leader's Guide

Interpretation Bible Studies (IBS), for adults and older youth, are flexible, attractive, easy-to-use, and filled with solid information about the Bible. IBS helps Christians discover the guidance and power of the scriptures for living today. Perhaps you are leading a church school class, a mid-week Bible study group, or a youth group meeting, or simply using this in your own personal study. Whatever the setting may be, we hope you find this *Leader's Guide* helpful. Since every context and group is different, this *Leader's Guide* does not presume to tell you how to structure Bible study for your situation. Instead, the *Leader's Guide* seeks to offer choices—a number of helpful suggestions for leading a successful Bible study using IBS.

> "The church that no longer hears the essential message of the Scriptures soon ceases to understand what it is for and is open to be captured by the dominant religious philosophy of the moment." —James D. Smart, *The Strange Silence of the Bible in the Church: A Study in Hermeneutics* (Philadelphia: Westminster Press, 1970), 10.

How Should I Teach IBS?

1. Explore the Format

There is a wealth of information in IBS, perhaps more than you can use in one session. In this case, more is better. IBS has been designed to give you a well-stocked buffet of content and teachable insights. Pick and choose what suits your group's needs. Perhaps you will want to split units into two or more sessions, or combine units into a single session. Perhaps you will decide to use only a portion of a unit and then move on to the next unit. *There is not a structured theme or teaching focus to each unit that must be followed for IBS to be used.* Rather, IBS offers the flexibility to adjust to whatever suits your context.

A recent survey of both professional and volunteer church educators revealed that their number-one concern was that Bible study materials be teacher-friendly. IBS is indeed teacher-friendly in two important ways. First, since IBS provides abundant content and a flexible design, teachers can shape the lessons creatively, responding to the needs of the group and employing a wide variety of teaching methods. Second, those who wish more specific suggestions for planning the sessions can find them at the Westminster John Knox Press Web site (**www.wjkbooks.com**). Here, you can access a study guide with teaching suggestions for each IBS unit as well as helpful quotations, selections from Bible dictionaries and encyclopedias, and other teaching helps.

> "The more we bring to the Bible, the more we get from the Bible." — William Barclay, *A Beginner's Guide to the New Testament* (Louisville, Ky.: Westminster John Knox Press, 1995), vii.

IBS is not only teacher-friendly, it is also discussion-friendly. Given the opportunity, most adults and young people relish the chance to talk about the kind of issues raised in IBS. The secret, then, is to determine what works with your group, what will get them to talk. Several good methods for stimulating discussion are presented in this *Leader's Guide,* and once you learn your group, you can apply one of these methods and get the group discussing the Bible and its relevance in their lives.

The format of every IBS unit consists of several features:

a. Body of the Unit. This is the main content, consisting of interesting and informative commentary on the passage and scholarly insight into the biblical text and its significance for Christians today.

b. Sidebars. These are boxes that appear scattered throughout the body of the unit, with maps, photos, quotations, and intriguing ideas. Some sidebars can be identified quickly by a symbol, or icon, that helps the reader know what type of information can be found in that sidebar. There are icons for illustrations, key terms, pertinent quotes, and more.

c. Want to Know More? Each unit includes a "Want to Know More?" section that guides learners who wish to dig deeper and consult other resources. If your church library does not have the resources mentioned, you can look up the information in other standard Bible dictionaries, encyclopedias, and handbooks, or you can find much of this information at the Westminster John Knox Press Web site (see last page of this Guide).

d. Questions for Reflection. The unit ends with questions to help the learners think more deeply about the biblical passage and its pertinence for today. These questions are provided as examples only, and teachers are encouraged both to develop their own list of questions and to gather questions from the group. These discussion questions do not usually have specific "correct" answers. Again, the

> "The trick is to make the Bible our book." —Duncan S. Ferguson, *Bible Basics: Mastering the Content of the Bible* (Louisville, Ky.: Westminster John Knox Press, 1995), 3.

flexibility of IBS allows you to use these questions at the end of the group time, at the beginning, interspersed throughout, or not at all.

2. Select a Teaching Method

Here are ten suggestions. The format of IBS allows you to choose what direction you will take as you plan to teach. Only you will know how your lesson should best be designed for your group. Some adult groups prefer the lecture method, while others prefer a high level of free-ranging discussion. Many youth groups like interaction, activity, the use of music, and the chance to talk about their own experiences and feelings. Here is a list of a few possible approaches. Let your own creativity add to the list!

a. Let's Talk about What We've Learned. In this approach, all group members are requested to read the scripture passage and the IBS unit before the group meets. Ask the group members to make notes about the main issues, concerns, and questions they see in the passage. When the group meets, these notes are collected, shared, and discussed. This method depends, of course, on the group's willingness to do some "homework."

b. What Do We Want and Need to Know? This approach begins by having the whole group read the scripture passage together. Then, drawing from your study of the IBS, you, as the teacher, write on a board or flip chart two lists:

(1) Things we should know to better understand this passage (content information related to the passage, for example, historical insights about political contexts, geographical landmarks, economic nuances, etc.), and

> "Although small groups can meet for many purposes and draw upon many different resources, the one resource which has shaped the life of the Church more than any other throughout its long history has been the Bible."—Roberta Hestenes, *Using the Bible in Groups* (Philadelphia: Westminster Press, 1983), 14.

(2) Four or five "important issues we should talk about regarding this passage" (with implications for today—how the issues in the biblical context continue into today, for example, issues of idolatry or fear).

Allow the group to add to either list, if they wish, and use the lists to lead into a time of learning, reflection, and discussion. This approach is suitable for those settings where there is little or no advanced preparation by the students.

c. Hunting and Gathering. Start the unit by having the group read the scripture passage together. Then divide the group into smaller clusters (perhaps having as few as one person), each with a different assignment. Some clusters can discuss one or more of the "Questions for Reflection." Others can look up key terms or people in a Bible dictionary or track down other biblical references found in the body of the unit. After the small clusters have had time to complete their tasks, gather the entire group again and lead them through the study material, allowing each cluster to contribute what it learned.

d. From Question Mark to Exclamation Point. This approach begins with contemporary questions and then moves to the biblical content as a response to those questions. One way to do this is for you to ask the group, at the beginning of the class, a rephrased version of one or more of the "Questions for Reflection" at the end of the study unit. For example, one of the questions at the end of the unit on Exodus 3:1–4:17 in the IBS *Exodus* volume reads,

> Moses raised four protests, or objections, to God's call. Contemporary people also raise objections to God's call. In what ways are these similar to Moses' protests? In what ways are they different?

This question assumes familiarity with the biblical passage about Moses, so the question would not work well before the group has explored the passage. However, try rephrasing this question as an opening exercise; for example:

Here is a thought experiment: Let's assume that God, who called people in the Bible to do daring and risky things, still calls people today to tasks of faith and courage. In the Bible, God called Moses from a burning bush and called Isaiah in a moment of ecstatic worship in the Temple. How do you think God's call is experienced by people today? Where do you see evidence of people saying "yes" to God's call? When people say "no" or raise an objection to God's call, what reasons do they give (to themselves, to God)?

Posing this or a similar question at the beginning will generate discussion and raise important issues, and then it can lead the group into an exploration of the biblical passage as a resource for thinking even more deeply about these questions.

e. Let's Go to the Library. From your church library, your pastor's library, or other sources, gather several good commentaries on the book of the Bible you are studying. Among the trustworthy commentaries are those in the Interpretation series (John Knox Press) and the Westminster Bible Companion series (Westminster John Knox Press). Divide your groups into smaller clusters and give one commentary to each cluster (one or more of the clusters can be given the IBS volume instead of a full-length commentary). Ask each cluster to read the biblical passage you are studying and then to read the section of the commentary that covers that passage (if your group is large, you may want to make photocopies of the commentary material with proper permission, of course). The task of each cluster is to name the two or three most important insights they discover about the biblical passage by reading and talking together about the commentary material. When you reassemble the larger group to share these insights, your group will gain not only a variety of insights about the passage but also a sense that differing views of the same text are par for the course in biblical interpretation.

f. Working Creatively Together. Begin with a creative group task, tied to the main thrust of the study. For example, if the study is on the Ten Commandments, a parable, or a psalm, have the group rewrite the Ten Commandments, the parable, or the psalm in contemporary language. If the passage is an epistle, have the group write a letter to their own congregation. Or if the study is a narrative, have the group role-play the characters in the story or write a page describing the story from the point of view of one of the characters. After completion of the task, read and discuss the biblical passage, asking for interpretations and applications from the group and tying in IBS material as it fits the flow of the discussion.

g. Singing Our Faith. Begin the session by singing (or reading) together a hymn that alludes to the biblical passage being studied (or to the theological themes in the passage). For example, if you are studying the unit from the IBS volume on Psalm 121, you can sing "I to the Hills Will Lift My Eyes," "Sing Praise to God, Who Reigns Above," or another hymn based on Psalm 121. Let the group reflect on the thoughts and feelings evoked by the hymn, then move to the biblical passage, allowing the biblical text and the IBS material to underscore, clarify, refine, and deepen the discussion stimulated by the hymn. If you are ambitious, you may ask the group to write a new hymn at the end of the study! (Many hymnals have indexes in the back or companion volumes that help the user match hymns to scripture passages or topics.)

h. Fill in the Blanks. In order to help the learners focus on the content of the biblical passage, at the beginning of the session ask each member of the group to read the biblical passage and fill out a brief questionnaire about the details of the passage (provide a copy for each learner or write the questions on the board). For example, if you are studying the unit in the IBS *Matthew* volume on Matthew 22:1–14, the questionnaire could include questions such as the following:

—In this story, Jesus compares the kingdom of heaven to what?
—List the various responses of those who were invited to the king's banquet but who did not come.
—When his invitation was rejected, how did the king feel? What did the king do?
—In the second part of the story, when the king saw a man at the banquet without a wedding garment, what did the king say? What did the man say? What did the king do?
—What is the saying found at the end of this story?

Gather the group's responses to the questions and perhaps encourage discussion. Then lead the group through the IBS material helping the learners to understand the meanings of these details and the significance of the passage for today. Feeling creative? Instead of a fill-in-the-blanks questionnaire, create a crossword puzzle from names and words in the biblical passage.

i. Get the Picture. In this approach, stimulate group discussion by incorporating a painting, photograph, or other visual object into the lesson. You can begin by having the group examine and comment on this visual or you can introduce the visual later in the lesson—it depends on the object used. If, for example, you are studying the unit Exodus 3:1–4:17 in the IBS *Exodus* volume, you may want to view Paul Koli's very colorful painting *The Burning Bush.* Two sources for this painting are *The Bible through Asian Eyes,* edited by Masao Takenaka and Ron O'Grady (National City, Calif.: Pace Publishing Co., 1991), and *Imaging the Word: An Arts and Lectionary Resource,* vol. 3, edited by Susan A. Blain (Cleveland: United Church Press, 1996).

j. Now Hear This. Especially if your class is large, you may want to use the lecture method. As the teacher, you prepare a presentation on the biblical passage, using as many resources as you have available plus your own experience, but following the content of the IBS unit as a guide. You can make the lecture even more lively by asking the learners at various points along the way to refer to the visuals and quotes found in the "sidebars." A place can be made for questions (like the ones at the end of the unit)—either at the close of the lecture or at strategic points along the way.

> "It is . . . important to call a Bible study group back to what the text being discussed actually says, especially when an individual has gotten off on some tangent." —Richard Robert Osmer, *Teaching for Faith: A Guide for Teachers of Adult Classes* (Louisville, Ky.: Westminster/John Knox Press, 1992), 71.

3. Keep These Teaching Tips in Mind

There are no surefire guarantees for a teaching success. However, the following suggestions can increase the chances for a successful study:

a. Always Know Where the Group Is Headed. Take ample time beforehand to prepare the material. Know the main points of the study, and know the destination. Be flexible, and encourage discussion, but don't lose sight of where you are headed.

b. Ask Good Questions; Don't Be Afraid of Silence. Ideally, a discussion blossoms spontaneously from the reading of the scripture. But more often than not, a discussion must be drawn from the group members by a series of well-chosen questions. After asking each question, give the group members time to answer. Let them think, and don't be threatened by a season of silence. Don't feel that every question must have an answer, and that as leader, you must supply every answer. Facilitate discussion by getting the group members to cooperate with each other. Sometimes the original question can be restated. Sometimes it is helpful to ask a follow-up question like "What makes this a hard question to answer?"

Ask questions that encourage explanatory answers. Try to avoid questions that can be answered simply "Yes" or "No." Rather than asking, "Do you think Moses was frightened by the burning bush?" ask, "What do you think Moses was feeling and experiencing as he stood before the burning bush?" If group members answer with just one word, ask a follow-up question like "Why do you think this is so?" Ask questions about their feelings and opinions, mixed within questions about facts or details. Repeat their responses or restate their response to reinforce their contributions to the group.

"Studies of learning reveal that while people remember approximately 10% of what they hear, they remember up to 90% of what they say. Therefore, to increase the amount of learning that occurs, increase the amount of talking about the Bible which each member does."—Roberta Hestenes, *Using the Bible in Groups* (Philadelphia: Westminster Press, 1983), 17.

Most studies can generate discussion by asking open-ended questions. Depending on the group, several types of questions can work. Some groups will respond well to content questions that can be answered from reading the IBS comments or the biblical passage. Others will respond well to questions about feelings or thoughts. Still others will respond to questions that challenge them to new thoughts or that may not have exact answers. Be sensitive to the group's dynamic in choosing questions.

Some suggested questions are: What is the point of the passage? Who are the main characters? Where is the tension in the story? Why does it say (this) _____, and not (that) _____? What raises questions for you? What terms need defining? What are the new ideas? What doesn't make sense? What bothers or troubles you about this passage? What keeps you from living the truth of this passage?

c. Don't Settle for the Ordinary. There is nothing like a surprise. Think of special or unique ways to present the ideas of the study. Upset the applecart of the ordinary. Even though the passage may be familiar, look for ways to introduce suspense. Remember that a little mystery can capture the imagination. Change your routine.

Along with the element of surprise, humor can open up a discussion. Don't be afraid to laugh. A well-chosen joke or cartoon may present the central theme in a way that a lecture would have stymied.

Sometimes a passage is too familiar. No one speaks up because everyone feels that all that could be said has been said. Choose an unfamiliar translation from which to read, or if the passage is from a Gospel, compare the story across two or more Gospels and note differences. It is amazing what insights can be drawn from seeing something strange in what was thought to be familiar.

d. Feel Free to Supplement the IBS Resources with Other Material. Consult other commentaries or resources. Tie in current events with the lesson. Scour newspapers or magazines for stories that touch on the issues of the study. Sometimes the lyrics of a song, or a section of prose from a well-written novel, will be just the right seasoning for the study.

e. And Don't Forget to Check the Web. You can download a free study guide from our Web site (**www.wjkbooks.com**). Each study guide includes several possibilities for applying the teaching methods suggested above for individual IBS units.

f. Stay Close to the Biblical Text. Don't forget that the goal is to learn the Bible. Return to the text again and again. Avoid making the mistake of reading the passage only at the beginning of the study, and then wandering away to comments on top of comments from that point on. Trust in the power

> "The Bible is literature, but it is much more than literature. It is the holy book of Jews and Christians, who find there a manifestation of God's presence." —Kathleen Norris, *The Psalms* (New York: Riverhead Books, 1997), xxii.

and presence of the Holy Spirit to use the truths of the passage to work within the lives of the study participants.

What If Am Using IBS in Personal Bible Study?

If you are using IBS in your personal Bible study, you can experiment and explore a variety of ways. You may choose to read straight through the study without giving any attention to the sidebars or other features. Or you may find yourself interested in a question or unfamiliar with a key term, and you can allow the sidebars "Want to

Know More?" and "Questions for Reflection" to lead you into deeper learning on these issues. Perhaps you will want to have a few commentaries or a Bible dictionary available to pursue what interests you. As was suggested in one of the teaching methods above, you may want to begin with the questions at the end, and then read the Bible passage followed by the IBS material. Trust the IBS resources to provide good and helpful information, and then follow your interests!

Want to Know More?

About leading Bible study groups? See Roberta Hestenes, *Using the Bible in Groups* (Philadelphia: Westminster Press, 1983).

About basic Bible content? See Duncan S. Ferguson, *Bible Basics: Mastering the Content of the Bible* (Louisville, Ky.: Westminster John Knox Press, 1995); William M. Ramsay, *The Westminster Guide to the Books of the Bible* (Louisville, Ky.: Westminster John Knox Press, 1994).

About the development of the Bible? See John Barton, *How the Bible Came to Be* (Louisville, Ky.: Westminster John Knox Press, 1997).

About the meaning of difficult terms? See Donald K. McKim, *Westminster Dictionary of Theological Terms* (Louisville, Ky.: Westminster John Knox Press, 1996); Paul J. Achtemeier, *Harper's Bible Dictionary* (San Francisco: Harper & Row, 1985).

To download a free IBS study guide,

visit our Web site at

www.wjkbooks.com